## Advance Praise for Les McKeown and *Predictable Success*

"*Predictable Success* provides an incredibly useful blueprint for any leader who is looking for sustainable growth."

—**Marshall Goldsmith,** million-selling author of *Succession: Are You Ready?* and *What Got You Here Won't Get You There*—a *WSJ* #1 bestseller

"Les really captures the integration of key business processes, people and leadership to consistently deliver a compelling vision, a comprehensive plan and profitable growth for the benefit of all stakeholders."

—**Alan Mulally,** president & CEO, Ford Motor Company

"*Predictable Success* isn't a textbook—it's a sensible and strategic playbook for any leader seeking to take their organization to the next level, and provides the conceptual framework to ensure a successful outcome."

—**David A. Brandon,** chairman and CEO, Domino's Pizza

"He's got it right. Les McKeown has uncovered the core dynamics of organizational growth, and mapped it to the best (and worst!) practices to achieve and maintain optimal, in-your-zone conditions—no matter where a group is in its evolution. This is real-world expertise, with simple but subtle and sophisticated prescriptions for all of us involved in getting things done with other people. And, oh yeah, he nailed how to address some key opportunities in my own company. *Predictable Success* should be required reading for every management team."

—**David Allen**, bestselling author, *Getting Things Done* and *Making It Work*

"Les McKeown is absolutely on top of his game. Les not only knows—and shows—how your businesses can grow and succeed, he explains it in a way that is intuitive, entertaining and immediately actionable."

—**Darryl Hutson,** American Express Incentive Services

"Les McKeown has for over seven years assisted us in the growth and development of our distributorship network. His understanding of what makes a business succeed—and his passionate commitment to teaching others how to accomplish Predictable Success—has been our secret weapon and can be yours, too."

—**Mel Haught,** CEO, Pella Corp

"Les McKeown clearly has a deep understanding of how businesses grow. His *Predictable Success* methodology is simple, intuitive and powerful."

—**Brian Walker**, president and CEO, Herman Miller Inc.

"This book has come at the perfect time. *Predictable Success* will completely change the way you think about growing your business. Absorb its ideas before your competitors do."

—**David McNally,** bestselling author of *Even Eagles Need a Push* and *The Eagle's Secret*

"*Predictable Success* provides a robust framework for any business leader wanting to achieve consistent and profitable growth. Les McKeown's real-world descriptions of company growth cycles should be heeded by all managers."

—**Vance Bell,** CEO Shaw Industries Inc (a Berkshire Hathaway company)

"Embracing change and using it positively is a fundamental requirement for growth in any organization, and the health care industry today is ripe for change in all sectors. In *Predictable Success*, Les McKeown provides simple, elegant, and effective tools for all leaders to understand why and how change occurs in their organizations, and teaches us how to harness that change to achieve success and competitive advantage in our fields. Les McKeown's ideas and insights are brilliantly written, entertaining, and easy to grasp and implement—no effective CEO or manager should miss this book!"

—**Dr. Wendy Everett**, President, New England Healthcare Institute

"It's difficult to predict success. Failure is far easier to predict because it's where most people end up. But if you want predictable success, then this book is for you. And, you might find that Les' formula for predicting success is not what you think."

—**Michael Port,** author of the *NY Times* bestseller, *The Think Big Manifesto*

"Les McKeown has an intuitive understanding of why and how business works. *Predictable Success* is practical and easy to understand—exactly what any executive needs to grow his business."

—**Keith Ferrazzi**, #1 *NY Times* bestselling author of *Never Eat Alone* and *Who's Got Your Back*

"I've experienced firsthand the positive impact and lasting change that Les McKeown's *Predictable Success* brings to a growing business—and to its leaders. If you want to structure your organization to get to the next stage in growth, and also want to develop personally as a leader, I strongly recommend you get started with *Predictable Success*."

—**Matt Long,** president, J.E. Higgins Group

"There is literally a smile, uncomfortable frown, or a holy crap! on each page."

—**Kevin Cassidy,** chairman, KC Company, Beltsville, Maryland

"*Predictable Success* is the 'ah-ha!' book. Les's insight and real-world stories are not only entertaining, they also clearly detail the different stages in the lifecycle of a company, and more importantly, how to avoid declining into 'treadmill' and 'death rattle.' A don't-miss business book!"

—**David Greer,** CEO, Wire Belt Company, Inc

"Les is the Butch Harmon of business consulting."

—**Graydon Bevis,** president, Pella Windows and Doors, Colorado

"Over the past three years, Les McKeown's *Predictable Success* has completely revolutionized how I and my team manage our business. Working with Les vastly accelerated our success and saved us from a multitude of potential 'dead ends.' I'm convinced our investment in *Predictable Success* has repaid itself many times over. I thoroughly recommend Les McKeown and the Predictable Success program for any business wanting to break through to the next stage in growth."

—**John Estabrook,** CEO, Horne Building Specialties, Inc.

# PREDICTABLE SUCCESS

[ GETTING YOUR ORGANIZATION ON THE
GROWTH TRACK—AND KEEPING IT THERE ]

## LES McKEOWN

GREENLEAF
BOOK GROUP PRESS

Published by Greenleaf Book Group Press
Austin, Texas
www.gbgpress.com

Distributed by Greenleaf Book Group LLC

For ordering information or special discounts for bulk purchases, please contact Greenleaf Book Group LLC at PO Box 91869, Austin, TX 78709, 512.891.6100.

Predictable Success is a registered trademark of EVNA Inc.

Design and composition by Greenleaf Book Group LLC
Cover design by Greenleaf Book Group LLC
Illustrations by neontetramedia

Publisher's Cataloging-In-Publication Data
(Prepared by The Donohue Group, Inc.)

McKeown, Les (John Leslie), 1956–
    Predictable success : getting your organization on the growth track--and keeping it there / Les McKeown. -- 1st ed.

    p. : ill. ; cm.

    Includes index.
    ISBN: 978-1-60832-031-8

1. Organizational change--Forecasting. 2. Success in business. 3. Industrial management. I. Title.

HD58.8 .M35 2010
658                                                                                  2009942923

Part of the Tree Neutral™ program, which offsets the number of trees consumed in the production and printing of this book by taking proactive steps, such as planting trees in direct proportion to the number of trees used: www.treeneutral.com. Printed in the United States of America on acid-free paper.

10 11 12 13 14   10 9 8 7 6 5 4 3 2 1

TreeNeutral

First Edition

# 〔 CONTENTS 〕

# [ FOREWORD ]

## WHY YOU SHOULD READ THIS BOOK

IN THIS BOOK I SHOW HOW ANY GROUP OF PEOPLE CAN REACH A state where they will consistently (and with relative ease) achieve their common goals—a state that I call "Predictable Success."

As you will discover, getting to Predictable Success is a practical, step-by-step process that is attainable by anyone. No special skills are required; no leap of faith is needed; there are no mantras to learn or secrets to divine. The principles of Predictable Success are simple, elegant and (once they've been pointed out) both obvious and natural. Because of this, there is little learning curve: Most people grasp the underlying concept and the main principles immediately.

In fact, as you read, you will discover that both intuitively and from your own past experiences you already know much of what is required to get to Predictable Success. If you work with a team or group, it is likely that you have already been practicing many of the principles of Predictable

Success subconsciously. This book will provide you with the methodology and additional knowledge you need to harness those insights, enabling you to consciously guide your team, group or organization into Predictable Success using a structured, accelerated process.

The principles of Predictable Success are universal. While for the sake of clarity I have chosen to write in the primary context of business, the principles of Predictable Success will work for any group, in any situation. If you head up or are part of a division or department, a project team, a not-for-profit, a government agency, a nongovernmental organization, a charity, a soccer team, a church committee or a family—any group of people who are trying to achieve something together—then Predictable Success is for you, and you will benefit from reading this book.

**Note:** The case histories found in this book are composites created from the hundreds of businesses I've worked with and learned from over the years. Any resemblance to a particular individual, living or deceased, or business situation is unintended and is purely coincidental.

# [ PREFACE ]

## UNCOVERING PREDICTABLE SUCCESS

MICHELANGELO SAID THAT THE JOB OF THE SCULPTOR WAS TO "free the forms that were already there"—that sculpting involves chipping away all that disguises the statue already hidden within the stone. By this definition, I've spent a lifetime "sculpting" Predictable Success: My career has been a process of chipping away the confusion, misinformation and presuppositions to uncover the true nature of success hidden beneath.

I've always been fascinated by the patterns of success: As a child I was intrigued by why certain kids were more popular in school, why each year one toy would become the must-have Christmas gift, why a specific sport or hobby would "go viral" in the neighborhood. Business in particular fascinated me. I loved it when my dad would take me into his office and I could wander around this strange landscape of desks and chairs and type-writers (yes, typewriters—it was that long ago). At the age of eleven, I had three part-time jobs: There was a milk delivery plant nearby and I would climb out of bed at 4:30 a.m. to go stand with other kids at the factory gates, where we would be hired each morning by milk delivery men to help them on their rounds; at 7:30 a.m. I would start my morning newspaper round; and at 4:00 p.m., I would begin my evening paper round. I was quite the little mogul.

I was intrigued by the comparative success of two local stores. Our local convenience store had been trading successfully in the same spot for as long as anyone could remember—generations, probably—but another shop just fifty feet away never seemed to succeed, despite a cycle of hopeful tenants, each doomed to failure as certain as the last. (I came up with an abstruse theory about traffic patterns and pedestrian flow.)

## My First Discovery

So in my late teenage years, when my father decided to leave the security of his office job and open—you guessed it—a local convenience store, I was excited at the possibility of learning more about how a real business (albeit a mini-business) worked. Unfortunately, the excitement didn't last long—the business failed within a year, and my parents had to declare bankruptcy.

For my mom and dad, I'm sure this must have been a painful, anguished time—they mostly hid that aspect from my sister and me—but they buckled down and worked their way out of it, and after a period during which we lived with my grandparents, life returned to relative normality.

For me, the experience was bewildering. Why had our little shop failed when tens—hundreds—of other similar stores were thriving around us? What did the owners of those stores know that we didn't? Was there something we should have done but hadn't? Was there something we didn't do that we should have? Intellectually, I was adrift—I didn't know how to analyze what had just happened. Worse, I didn't even know where to start.

Partly as a result of this bewilderment, partly because of the financial constraints the business collapse had caused, and partly because of advice I received, I dropped my college plans (I had intended to study journalism) and instead entered into a five-year articleship to become a chartered accountant—the British equivalent of a CPA. I thought that a solid grounding in accounting would fill the gaps in my understanding about what made businesses succeed or fail.

During those five years, I began for the first time to chip away at my understanding of what makes for success in business. I spent days, weeks, months—in offices, attics, basements, showrooms, lumber yards, factories and warehouses—poring over general ledgers, analyzing accounts receivable, counting inventories, registering assets and estimating liabilities. I learned about cash flow, profit margins, liquidity, balance sheet strength, return on investment, price/earnings ratios and working capital. I loved every minute of it. I studied like a demon, and in my two-part finals I came first in Ireland. Basking in the glow of success, I moved to London for a year, where I worked for one of the "big eight" accounting firms (as they were then), to experience what it was like to audit enormous, multinational companies.

When I returned to Ireland to join an accounting and consulting firm as a partner at just twenty-three, I believed I had unlocked the mystery of business success. It was simple: If you got the numbers right, everything else would follow. We accountants had the secret of business success—we just weren't that good at explaining it. I decided my personal path to success was to become the best communicator the accounting profession would ever see. I not only knew the secret of business success, but I would now explain it to anyone who wanted to hear—for a fee.

For nine years, I expounded my newfound knowledge for my long-suffering clients, and at their expense I honed my ability to "get the numbers right," first in the firm I had joined when I returned to Ireland, then five years later when I struck out on my own. I became more and more hands-on, not just helping my clients interpret their results once a year, but meeting with them regularly and helping them proactively shape their balance sheet, profit and loss accounts, and cash flows.

Increasingly, clients began to recommend me to their friends and peers. I gained a reputation as the accountant of choice for anyone thinking of starting a business, and I began to specialize in helping people set up new ventures. Eventually I dropped the compliance work (accounts and tax preparation) entirely, to concentrate solely on my consulting clients.

People began to ask me to take a more active role in their start-ups. Sometimes a couple of entrepreneurs would approach me with an idea but no money; sometimes they had the money but no business concept. I started to selectively identify new ventures that I was interested in and that I thought would succeed, and I would agree to act as cofounder in those that passed my "it's all in the numbers" test.

# Hmm—Maybe There's More to It Than That . . .

In the space of five years, I took an active role in the launch of forty-two companies, including such diverse businesses as a tool and die manufacturer, a PR agency, a graphic design agency and a computer training company. I bought the Pizza Hut Master Franchise for Ireland and with my partner committed to opening twenty restaurants. I sold my interest in most of these businesses back to the other founders over time. A few failed, most continued as small business providing a good living for their owners, and some went on to great success.

And I discovered something very interesting.

In this frenzy of new venturing, I had (albeit unwittingly) chipped away another piece of stone and moved considerably closer to understanding the true cause of success. What I found out was this: It isn't about the numbers.

Sure, having a well-funded business with good financial management doesn't do any harm. But in getting my hands dirty with real businesses for the first time, it became clear that simply getting the numbers right—having a strong balance sheet, good cash flow, good profitability—isn't in itself an indicator of success. Put simply: A lot of well-financed businesses still go under. (Twenty years later, the dot-com bubble would underline this point.)

I watched seemingly well-financed businesses go under for reasons that on the surface looked unconnected—overconfident sales projections, poor salesmanship, lack of commitment, overinvestment in assets being just a few. But when I analyzed the reasons in more depth, a pattern began to emerge: It wasn't the numbers. It was the *people* that made the ultimate difference between success and failure.

With that, another piece of stone fell away. The statue I was carving (I didn't have a name for it then, but "Predictable Success" would come later) was beginning to form a shape—blurry, incomplete—but a shape, nonetheless. And the shape so far revealed that business success—true, lasting business success—came not from a well-structured balance sheet and good financial management—but from the *people*. If you didn't have the right people, it was only a matter of time before the money would run out.

It was time to chip some more.

## Wholesaling Predictable Success

In 1991, I was approached by a former client to join him in a wacky idea. The concept was to develop a training program to teach people how to launch new businesses. That wasn't the wacky part—it was really just wholesaling what I was doing as a consultant on a retail basis. The wacky part was that this program would be run in West Belfast, then a highly dangerous flashpoint during one of the most murderous periods of the "Troubles" in Northern Ireland.

Not surprisingly, West Belfast had a horrendous unemployment problem, and the Entrepreneurship Program (as it was to be known) was an attempt to help reduce the unemployment rate in the area. The upside was that the UK government was heavily subsidizing the program. They were prepared to pay my partner and I well—very well—and in what I hoped wasn't a commentary on just how dangerous the area was, they were prepared to pay our fee 100 percent up front. I took the gig.

The Entrepreneurship Program was an out-of-the-park success. My partner and I worked hard at both the curriculum and the training itself, and after a couple of cohorts had moved through the program, we had the whole process down. In keeping with my evolving model, we became very good at picking the right people for the program and making sure that they were as well funded as possible, often using some of the government money that was available for the area. The program exceeded every metric that was set for it, and within a year, my partner and I were being approached by other agencies throughout the UK to do something similar.

Over the next decade, we ran versions of the Entrepreneurship Program from incubation units across the UK, launching hundreds of business that would eventually employ thousands of employees. The program won the prestigious European Union Job Challenge Award, and we built other business development programs, eventually operating in Canada, the US, Singapore, Paris and Dubai.

This international dimension gave me a unique opportunity to observe how businesses grew and developed in different cultures, which in turn helped me separate the transcendent, overarching principles of business success from those that were merely temporal, or geographically or culturally specific.

Then another large piece of stone fell off, revealing something very interesting.

What happened was this: For a few years, we launched wave after wave of new businesses, founded—as much as possible—on the twin precepts of being well funded *and* involving the right people. And of course, after two or three years of launching new businesses, and certainly by years four, five, six and beyond, we were no longer working with just "new" businesses—our early launchees were now fully fledged, mature or maturing businesses.

Some of them began to fail. Even though we believed we had the right people and good financing, some of the businesses began to shudder and stall. Sometimes the original founders would need to be replaced (or wanted to be replaced), sometimes we needed to bring in an additional senior executive to get the business through the "shuddering" and out the other end, and sometimes the business would just plain fail.

## Chipping Off the Final Pieces

I felt as though I were right back in my parents' little convenience store. What was happening here? Why were the twin precepts—well financed, right people—not enough? What had I missed? Or worse, what was I doing that I shouldn't?

Again, after some analysis, the answer became obvious.

It's not the numbers. It's not even the numbers and the people. It's the numbers, the people *and the structure they operate in*. The numbers—and more important, the people—have to work within a vibrant, organic, dynamically changing organization. Structures that had worked well for our start-ups weren't holding up as the businesses grew larger. More important, oftentimes the founder/owner(s) either couldn't see the need to change the structure, didn't have the ability to change the structure, or simply didn't want to change the structure.

With this final chip falling off, I could now see the full outline of the sculpture. It didn't take long to figure out that the situation I had identified (that the *structure* needed to change between start-up and maturity) was highly likely to be only one of a series of changes that every organization would need to make as it got bigger and more complex. It seemed to me probable that there was a specific sequence of structural shifts over time that any successful organization—in fact, as I was to discover, any successful group—had to go through.

It was now just a matter of decoding that sequence.

## Honing the Model

By then, in 1999, I was sending an increasing amount of time in the United States, managing our business interests there. I had fallen in love: with Marin County, just outside San Francisco, and more important, with a woman who lived there and who would eventually become my wife. I decided to sell my interests in the consulting and other businesses I had back in the UK, and I moved to Marin, committed to polishing and honing the sculpture—to do whatever was needed to fully understand what I was beginning to call "Predictable Success."

I read everything I could find that dealt with business life cycles, attended workshops and seminars that helped me understand more about what I was discovering, and wrote, taught and consulted on the subject—always returning to the same touchstone, to my experiences with the hundreds upon hundreds of businesses I had helped launch and the more than forty that I personally cofounded. Eventually, the model you will read about in this book emerged, fully formed.

For the last ten years I have had the privilege of working alongside inspirational leaders in for-profit and not-for-profit organizations in every imaginable industry and sector, helping them inject Predictable Success into their organizations. I wrote this book to make the Predictable Success methodology available to a wider audience than I can reach through my teaching and consulting. I sincerely trust you'll enjoy reading this book as much as I've enjoyed writing it.

For me, it's the culmination of a lifetime's work helping leaders grow both themselves and their organizations.

For you, I hope it is just the start.

# [ INTRODUCTION ]

## WHAT PREDICTABLE SUCCESS IS, AND WHY YOU SHOULD CARE

PREDICTABLE SUCCESS IS A STATE REACHABLE BY ANY GROUP OF people—any organization, business, division, department, project, or team—in which they will consistently (and with relative ease) achieve their common goals.

Those of us who manage groups of people want to get to Predictable Success for a simple reason: It's much easier to manage a group when you—and they—know how to be successful. Just as it's easier to manage a football team that already knows how to win, and just as it's easier to come down the back nine on a Sunday afternoon at the Masters when you've already won fifteen majors, any group that knows how to succeed has a substantial competitive advantage over those that don't.

Managing an organization that is in any state other than Predictable Success is a trial of nerves: The organization may or may not be successful (you can't tell with any certainty in advance), and even when it is successful, it's hard to tell why or to "capture" that success so that it can be repeated.

# Does Your Car Move When You Step on the Gas Pedal?

The percentage of organizations that reach the stage of Predictable Success is small. Jeffrey Immelt, CEO of GE, said, "When you put your foot on the gas in this company, the car goes forward." While that might sound like a vacuous truism, the reality is that the leaders of most organizations can't say any such thing. For them, when they step on the gas pedal, the car may or may not go forward. And if it does go forward, it may or may not go in the direction they expected or desired.

For many business leaders, even when they do succeed in getting the car to move forward for a time, they live with the constant, subconscious fear that the car might stop again at any time. Ever had that sinking feeling when you unexpectedly run out of gas while barreling down the freeway? When, despite the fact that you've pushed the gas pedal to the floor, the car begins to decelerate and comes eventually to a shuddering stop?

For many owners and managers—for most of them, in fact—this is the reality they face: Each day, experimentation, hope and determination meet the unknown and the unexpected, and with luck, as a result, the car might go forward. And if doesn't go forward today, maybe it'll go forward tomorrow. Perhaps it will move in the right direction, and perhaps for more than a short period of time. Who knows?

Only leaders whose organizations are in Predictable Success can wake up every day and say, "When I put my foot on the gas in this company, the car goes forward." This book shows you how to be such a leader: how to take your organization, business, division, department, project, group or team into Predictable Success, and how to keep it there.

# So Why Isn't Everyone in Predictable Success?

If it is so much easier to run an organization when it is in Predictable Success, why do so few businesses, divisions, departments, projects, groups or teams ever get there? Why don't more of us who are business founders, owners, leaders and managers take the steps necessary to get the groups of people for which we are responsible into Predictable Success?

The reason is a bizarre but simple one: Nobody ever told us such a thing existed. Most of us (and I assume as you are reading this that I can count you as one of "us") were never told that success could be learned and replicated, understood and scaled, nurtured and sustained.

We were told about cash flow, human resources, people management, vendor selection, discount pricing, strategies and tactics, five P's and Six Sigmas—and a thousand other nuggets of information. But we were never shown how all of it could (and should) add up to more than fleeting or momentary or seasonal success: how we could, if we took the right steps, develop a type of success that could be replicated over time and in any environment. Put simply: We were given the tools *for* success and an expectation *of* success, but no dependable way of combining the two to consistently *achieve* success.

Because of this missing link—no dependable connection between the tools we have and the results we want—our experience in creating and sustaining success tends to be patchy: Sometimes stuff works, sometimes it doesn't. Sometimes the car goes forward, sometimes it doesn't. And this isn't an isolated experience—look at the titles on the shelves of the business section at your local bookstore next time you're browsing, and you'll see how universal the elusiveness of business success is.

As a result, as business owners and managers we have developed a collective belief system that throbs along in the background while we work, telling us that business success will just "happen" eventually if we do the right things (whatever they are). This belief system persuades us that while success is there, it is out of reach, locked up in a vault, waiting for us to crack the code. If we put in enough work, if we spend each day trying different combinations on the lock, one day, if we're lucky or prescient, we'll guess right, the tumblers will fall, the safe door will swing open and success will be ours.

## Here Is the Combination

Part of that underlying belief system is true. There is a code that will unlock success, predictably and consistently, in any organization. The part that is untrue is that you have to guess at what that code is, or that you have to experiment every day to get it right. The code for Predictable Success, on the other hand, is sitting in plain view and is available to anyone who wants to pick it up and use it. It's contained in this book.

You don't need to experiment day in, day out to find out how to make your organization predictably successful. Organizations have been in existence for long enough, and in enough numbers, that the patterns of organizational success and failure are as clear as the night sky, if you know where to look.

In this book, I'll show you where to look, what to look for and how to interpret what you see.

## The Structure of This Book

I've set out the path to Predictable Success for any organization, in two parts: Part 1 describes step by step the progression that every organization makes through each of the seven life cycle stages leading up to and away from Predictable Success. Part 2 discusses in detail the specific steps you need to take to move your organization into Predictable Success, and how to keep it there.

To view it another way: In Part 1, I'll show you the "what" of Predictable Success—what Predictable Success is, what the stages are that an organization goes through to get there, and what happens to an organization (or a business, division, department, project, group or team) once it arrives at Predictable Success. I'll also show you what happens to an organization if and when it "overshoots" Predictable Success and starts to age and decline.

In Part 2, you will discover the "how" of Predictable Success—you will learn how to establish precisely where your organization (or business, division, department, project, group or team) is along the road to Predictable Success, how to get there, and once there, how to stay there.

**Addendum:** Recently it has become common to encourage readers of business books to "dip in" to the text wherever they fancy—to cherry-pick those parts that capture their interest and leave the others. This is not such a book. You will be rewarded for working sequentially through the sections in turn.

## PART 1

## TAKING THE JOURNEY: HAVING A MAP MEANS
## YOU KNOW WHERE YOU'RE GOING

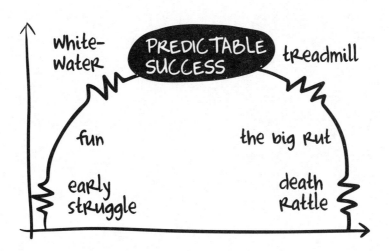

# [ CHAPTER ONE ]

## OVERVIEW: WHAT PREDICTABLE SUCCESS LOOKS LIKE FROM 30,000 FEET

WHEN I ARRIVED FOR MY FIRST MEETING WITH MIKE, HE SHOWED me into his conference room. "Too many distractions in my office," he explained. As it turned out, the conference room provided little relief. His assistant skittered in and out throughout our meeting—with papers to sign, questions to answer, documents needing approval. Three or four times, one or another of Mike's managers would peek around the door, asking for clarifications, conveying tidbits of information. Occasionally, the phone in the conference room would ring as yet another employee tracked Mike down. Maybe we should have met at the local Starbucks instead.

Mike had asked me to meet with him to explore the reasons why his company's growth had stalled over the previous eighteen months. As Mike was the founder and CEO of a 125-person paint distribution business, I understood that his attention might be needed by a colleague at some point in our ninety-minute meeting, but this was clearly abnormal. As the meeting went on, however, it became clear that what I was watching was more important than anything Mike was telling me. His organization had hit what I had come to call "Whitewater"—the company had outgrown its youthful, "turn on a dime," freewheeling culture, and desperately needed some processes and systems to bring order to the chaos that was slowly engulfing Mike and his managers.

As we worked through the questions I had for Mike, took a tour of his facility and met with some of his key people, everything I saw and heard confirmed that Mike had indeed hit Whitewater—big time. We scheduled our next meeting a month ahead, allowing Mike time to send me some data on his last four quarters' operations, and I promised to come back with my recommendations on the best way forward.

A couple of weeks later, I met with Gloria, VP of Sales for the consumer division of a national financial services company. The setting couldn't have been more different from my meeting with Mike. After a clockwork-precise guided tour of the two floors of quietly humming cubicles that were her domain, and a brief introduction to her boss, Gloria steered me into one of the tidiest, calmest offices I've ever seen. With no interruptions, and with every relevant document to hand and reproduced in glowing color, spiral-bound and dancing with charts and analysis, Gloria and I delved into the exact same problem as Mike's—why her sales had plateaued after seventeen straight quarters of unbroken growth, even though the industry as a whole was healthy.

As we ground through the data, Gloria choreographed a mini-ballet of presentations by her three lieutenants, each one with impeccable dress sense, impressive presentation skills and a strong grasp of the underlying data.

As I watched Gloria interact with her managers, I noticed the stylized manner in which the discussions took place—with acronyms and industry-speak used as shorthand, questions posed rhetorically, and much of the conversation sounding stilted, even rehearsed. Again, as with Mike, the evidence was clear just by watching what was going on—Gloria's division had hit "Treadmill," a later stage in organizational growth where process and systems had taken over, squeezing out creativity and risk taking. Individual meetings with each of her three managers confirmed it: Analysis of data had taken the place of honest debate, and personal initiative and innovation had given way to conformity, uniformity and fear of making mistakes. They were firmly in the grip of Treadmill.

At our roundup meeting at the end of the day, I gave Gloria the Web link for an assessment I wanted her and her managers to complete, and scheduled our second meeting one month ahead. As with Mike, I promised that at our next meeting we'd start looking at some answers to her problem.

Three days later, I stepped out of the blistering Midwest heat into the welcome, air-conditioned relief of a squat, four-story office block sitting at the entrance to an industrial park. I was here to meet with Phil, after an absence of six months. Phil had first called me when his snack brand company had acquired the ailing potato chip manufacturer whose offices I was now standing in, and Phil had been sent down from HQ to manage the division, with the goal of restoring profitability within twenty-four months. I'd worked with Phil and his team for those two years, and I was excited to have the chance to return and assess the results of our work together.

The stated reason I was there was to facilitate Phil's biannual "state of the business" meeting with his managers. While he was perfectly capable of chairing the meeting himself, Phil liked the freedom to participate without the responsibilities of chairmanship. He also liked bringing in someone with an outside perspective and who would not be afraid to ask dumb questions when necessary. I was pleased that he'd asked me to take on the role for this particular session.

I'd prepared myself for a long day of presentations, and I had assumed that each manager would be "reporting in" (or "reporting out") one by one. Maybe there would be some questions or a discussion or two, but mostly I was expecting the series of one-sided monologues that usually form the core of gatherings such as these. What I got instead was something very different. Sure, there were some presentations, but they were short and succinct, and were followed by incisive, focused discussions, usually two or three times longer than the presentation itself, and always building on the content of the presentation rather than reanalyzing or second-guessing it. The agenda was used merely as a jumping-off point for discussion, as the group probed and prodded the issues facing them, seemingly never content until they had held every issue up to the light and turned it in each direction, seeking always to add a new perspective or find a new answer.

It very quickly became obvious that this was no routine meeting to be endured before getting back to the "real" work at hand. Somehow, in that quiet conference room, undisturbed and intently focused, Phil and his managers seemed to summon the very lifeblood of their business into reality. Like master architects huddled around a set of blueprints, it was as if they could "see" the finished building; with every discussion it felt as though we were taking a virtual walk around the parts of the business we were reviewing. The people, processes and activities we discussed came alive as each manager drew on his or her experience and knowledge to enrich the discussion.

As I watched them in action, I realized that the group had developed an internal rhythm that paced their discussions. With each agenda item, the process was the same: They'd first gather the required information, usually already included in their pre-meeting materials, which everyone had read and which they didn't rehash, unless someone had a specific question. They would then debate the issue for as long as was necessary, always honestly and without defensiveness or blame or guilt. Finally, and swiftly, they would make a decision or, occasionally, defer the matter to a subgroup or a later meeting. It was the rhythm of effective and efficient decisionmaking, and as we moved into the afternoon I began to hear it drum in my mind: *Data, Debate, Decide or Defer . . . Data, Debate, Decide or Defer.*

When the time came to make decisions on each agenda item, the dynamic of the group shifted once more. It felt as if the room became an operating theater, with the managers donning scrubs and gathering together around the patient. For a short period, the level of focus and intensity shifted up a gear, with Phil acting as a first among equals, guiding but not dominating the decision-making process. The managers spoke clearly and precisely to each other, trading pieces of information as if reading vital signs from a heart monitor, all focused on one thing—the absolute health of their patient, their business. There were no personal agendas being pursued, no self-serving comments—just a shared desire to do the very best for the organization as a whole.

As the afternoon swept by, the agenda was knocked down item by item in the same relentless, effective rhythm, yet all was done with humor and time for occasional digressions. Finally the last agenda item was done. Phil checked that we had captured all the salient action points, and with that the meeting was over.

During the all-staff barbecue held later in the cool of the evening, I compared notes with Phil, and the next day, I circled through each of the the managers, meeting their teams and getting progress reports on how things had gone since we last had met, six months previously. It became clear that Phil had achieved exactly what Mike and Gloria so desired—he had brought his organization to the pinnacle of organizational growth. His organization wasn't perfect—no organization ever can be—and he still had challenges, many of them. But he also had a well-oiled, efficient, yet very human "machine" taking on those challenges. His organization and the people who ran it were "in the zone": Like an all-conquering football team winning the championship year after year, they had found a winning formula, one which Mike and Gloria craved. They had reached the state of development that I call Predictable Success.

On the plane ride home, tired but energized by my time with Phil and his team, I grabbed a yellow pad and began jotting some notes for my upcoming meetings with Mike and Gloria. Despite their deep concerns and the obvious challenges they faced, I was excited for them both. If they were up for it, Mike and Gloria—and the organizations they ran— were about to begin a transformative, challenging journey of discovery and development. It was the same journey that Phil had successfully com- pleted over the last thirty months, the same journey that I had had the privilege of witnessing—and facilitating—so many times before.

As I thought back on my first meetings with Mike and Gloria, I recalled how frustrated and impotent they felt. It was understandable: From their perspective, their organizations were mired in the mud, going nowhere. In fact, Mike—though he could barely bring himself to say it—feared for the very existence of his company. "I'm worried that we're not going to make it," he'd said to me. "I've never known a time when I've felt less in control of my company. I feel as though it's running me, not the other way around. If I can't get the business back on track soon, I'm seriously think- ing of selling out."

For Gloria, the issue was more personal. "Les," she'd said, "maybe I've got to accept that I've reached the limit of my management skills. Maybe I just don't have what it takes to take this division to the next level. I'm not sure I'm the right person for the job anymore."

Two very different people, two very different organizations, two different sets of challenges—yet they shared one important characteristic, and that shared characteristic was the cause of my optimism. Despite the different challenges and issues they faced, if they responded to those challenges in the right way, they were each in fact just one step away from reaching the peak of organizational development—the stage Phil and his team had reached: Predictable Success.

Granted, Mike and Gloria were each approaching Predictable Success from different directions—Mike with a more youthful organization coming "up" the growth curve, and Gloria managing a much larger enterprise trying hard not to slide "down." And yes, each (as we will see) would need to take very different—often symmetrically opposite—steps to get there, but their goal was identical: to get their respective organizations to a place where growth was once more attainable and, more important, sustainable. In other words, to achieve Predictable Success.

## What Predictable Success Is Not

What did Phil and his organization have that Mike's and Gloria's lacked? What does it mean for an organization to be in Predictable Success?

Well, let's start by defining what it is not:

**It's not about size.** Small organizations can be in Predictable Success, large organizations, too. A twenty-three-person firm of attorneys I work with is in Predictable Success; General Electric was for many years in Predictable Success while employing more than 300,000 people. Other organizations never get there, irrespective of how big they grow. Any organization, of any size, can be in Predictable Success if managed correctly.

**It's not about age.** Being in Predictable Success has nothing to do with the chronological age of organizations—a young organization can be in Predictable Success, and some very old organizations never get there. Litle & Co, a credit-card payment processing company, was number one on the Inc. 500 just five years after it was founded. SC Johnson regularly appears in *Fortune* magazine's Top 100 Companies to Work For and is more than 120 years old.

**It's not about money or other resources**. As the meltdown of fall 2008 proved all too clearly, resource-rich organizations cannot buy their way into Predictable Success. Conversely, if they take the right steps, resource-challenged organizations can make it to Predictable Success (and in doing so, will also resolve their resource needs faster than they would have otherwise). Microsoft has billions of dollars in its coffers, yet it is not in Predictable Success. A graphic design company I know is in Predictable Success despite funding itself from the partners' credit cards.

**It's not a culture.** Predictable Success is not about adopting any one organizational "culture." Organizations in Predictable Success don't all adopt the same way of doing business, use the same management style or follow the same "gurus." They each have a unique way of doing business that is specific to their own culture and goals. Predictable Success organizations can be highly disciplined, or looser and more freewheeling. They can be for-profit or not-for-profit, family oriented or more "corporate" in style—it doesn't matter.

**It's not about how meetings are held**. Although you can tell a lot about any organization by watching how its meetings are conducted (as I did with Mike, Gloria and Phil), this is an effect, not a cause. Meetings in Predictable Success organizations are run a certain way because they are in Predictable Success, not the other way around.

**It's not about the industry you're in**. I've worked with defense contractors, health care consultants, car parts manufacturers, software designers, government agencies, food distributors and everything in between. Predictable Success is entirely industry-neutral.

Okay—now we know a few things that Predictable Success is not. Let's turn now to what Predictable Success is:

# Predictable Success as a Natural Stage in Organizational Development

Look at Figure 1.1 below. Don't worry about understanding all the terms on the diagram—we'll get to those in due course. You can see that Predictable Success is one of the *seven stages of growth and decline* through which every organization progresses. Not every organization makes it all the way through all seven stages—some organizations stop at one or more stages; some make it to one stage, then drop back to the previous stage or stages; and some organizations die at a certain stage.

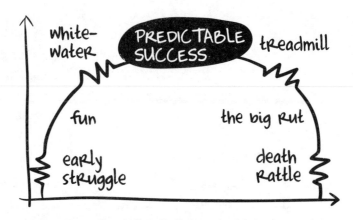

Figure 1.1 The Predictable Success Growth Cycle

Predictable Success is the apex of the growth curve. This book is about how to get there. The three stages before Predictable Success (Early Struggle, Fun and Whitewater) are *growth* stages. The stages after Predictable Success (Treadmill, The Big Rut and Death Rattle) are *decline* stages.

There are three important things to note about the growth cycle:

1. **Organizations cannot "jump" a stage.** For example, it's not possible to move into Predictable Success directly from Fun, bypassing Whitewater, no more than it's possible to jump from childhood to adulthood while bypassing puberty. Every organization trying to get to Predictable Success will move through Early Struggle, Fun and Whitewater at some point. However, by taking the right steps, it is possible to minimize the time spent in a specific stage.

2. **Organizations can move back as well as forward in the growth cycle**. For example, it is possible (and quite common) for an organization to cycle in and out of Whitewater and Fun a number of times. As we'll see, this is the fate of most organizations that do not take a planned approach to attaining Predictable Success.

3. **It is possible for an organization to remain in Predictable Success indefinitely**. By implementing the right strategies, any organization, division, department, group or team can undergo a process of continuous rejuvenation, allowing it to stay in Predictable Success and not decline either back into Whitewater or forward into Treadmill. Part 2 of this book explains how to achieve this.

# Hold On Tight: Predictable Success in 3 Minutes or Less

The chapters in Part 1 of this book describe each of the seven stages of the growth cycle in detail; however, if you have managed an organization of any size for any reasonable length of time, you may already have intuitively grasped the concepts behind each stage in the cycle. Here's a brief "helicopter ride" through the Predictable Success growth cycle. See how many stages you can recognize from your own experience:

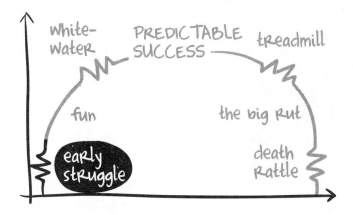

**Early Struggle.** It feels as if you're hacking through the jungle, fighting to keep your newborn organization alive. The two main challenges are (1)

making sure there is enough cash to keep going, until (2) you've clearly established that there is a market for your product or service.

The mortality rate of organizations is high in this stage—more than two-thirds of all organizations don't make it out of Early Struggle. You're fighting for your organization's very existence.

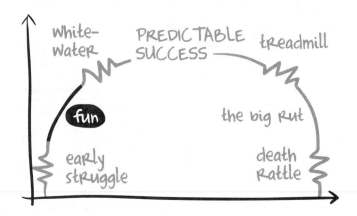

**Fun.** You've broken through the Early Struggle—you have cash (at least enough to take the pressure off) and an established market. It's time to have Fun! Now you're free to concentrate on getting your product or service into the market, so the key focus now moves from cash to sales.

This is the time when the organization's myths and legends are built, and the "Big Dogs" emerge—those loyal high producers who build the business exponentially in this time of rapid, first-stage growth.

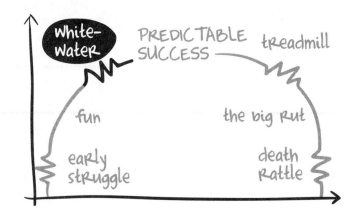

**Whitewater.** The very success that you reaped in the Fun stage brings with it the seeds of Whitewater: Your organization becomes complex, and the key emphasis shifts once more, from sales to profitability. Achieving sustained, profitable growth requires you to put in place consistent processes, policies and systems.

Unfortunately, putting those systems in place proves harder than you expected. Making the right decisions seems easy, but implementing decisions and making them stick is incredibly difficult. The organization seems to be going through an identity crisis, and you may even be doubting your leadership and management skills.

**Predictable Success.** You've developed a team that has successfully navigated your organization through Whitewater—congratulations! You have reached the prime stage in your organization's growth: Predictable Success.

Here, you can set (and consistently achieve) your goals and objectives with a consistent, predictable degree of success. Unlike Fun (when you were growing, but weren't quite sure how or why), in Predictable Success you know why you are successful, and you can use that information to sustain growth in the long term.

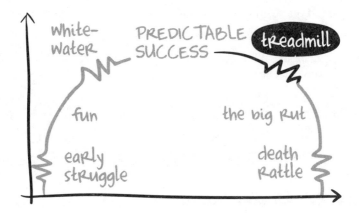

**Treadmill.** In principle, there is no reason for any organization to decline from the position of Predictable Success. In practice, many organizations begin to swing too far toward dependence on process and policies. Creativity, risk taking and initiative decline in response, and the organization becomes increasingly formulaic and arthritic.

Working for the organization at this stage in its development can feel like being on a Treadmill: A lot of energy is being expended, but there's little sense that forward momentum is being achieved. There's an overemphasis on data over action, on form over content. Good people start to leave—many of whom have been with the organization for some time. Even the entrepreneurial founder(s) (if they're still there) may be becoming frustrated and threatening to leave also.

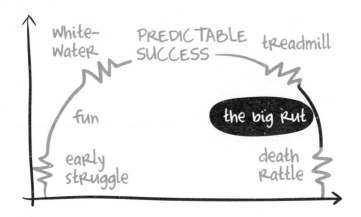

**The Big Rut.** Treadmill is a dangerous stage in the organization's development. If it is checked in time, creativity, risk taking and flexibility can be re-injected, taking the organization back to Predictable Success. Left unchecked, however, the organization will decline further into The Big Rut.

At this stage, process and administration have become more important than action and results. Worse, the organization loses its ability to be self-aware and cannot diagnose its own sickness and decline. When an organization reaches The Big Rut, it can stay there for a long time on a very gradual decline.

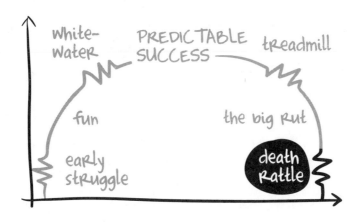

**Death Rattle.** Eventually, for all bureaucracies, there is a final attempt to resuscitate the organization, whether by the appointment of bankruptcy practitioners or by being acquired. Either way, the organization will not survive in its present form. After a brief Death Rattle (when illusory signs of life may be seen), the organization dies in its present form.

# The 5 Key Benefits of Achieving Predictable Success

So we've seen what it means from a technical perspective to be in Predictable Success, and we've taken a brief helicopter ride through the journey leading up to (and away) from it. Now let's see what it means, in reality, to actually be there. What is it like to manage or work in an organization that has reached Predictable Success?

Any organization that is in Predictable Success exhibits five main characteristics that, taken together, distinguish it from organizations at other stages in the growth cycle:

1. **Decision making.** The ability to readily make and consistently implement decisions.

2. **Goal setting.** The ability to readily set and consistently achieve goals.

3. **Alignment.** Structure, process and people are in harmony.

4. **Accountability.** Employees become self-accountable, in addition to being externally accountable to others.

5. **Ownership.** Employees take personal responsibility for their actions and outcomes.

Note that these characteristics are not "tidy"—they don't all begin with the same letter or spell out an easy acronym—they don't even roll easily off the tongue. That's because Predictable Success isn't a "made up" theory—it's an intuitive, natural reflection of the way things really are in predictably successful organizations—and sometimes, reality just refuses to be neat and tidy.

Let's take a look at each of the five Predictable Success characteristics in turn:

# 1. Decision Making: The Ability to Readily Make and Consistently Implement Decisions.

Spend any time with an organization in Predictable Success, and the first thing you'll notice is the way in which its members make decisions—particularly in comparison to organizations in Whitewater or Treadmill. There is neither the sense of sitting atop barely managed chaos that accompanies Whitewater, nor the plodding, turgid, rote decision making so often seen in Treadmill. Instead, there is a sense of *flow*—decisions are made without the decision-making process placing a burden on the organization. Sizing up an issue, crafting an appropriate response and getting it implemented doesn't slow down the day-to-day management activities.

Instead, decision making is an integral part of the management process—it happens naturally, organically, and is accepted not only by senior managers but by lower-level managers, team leaders and supervisors as just "part of the job." As Phil said at the barbecue when I shared with him my observations on seeing his team make decisions together, "That's what we come here to do every day, so we better be good at it."

And it's not just "command and control," centralized decision making either. In the Predictable Success organization, much—make that most—of the decision making is delegated and decentralized, freeing managers at all levels of the organization to concentrate on what they can do best, rather than micromanaging others. We'll see more on the impact of decentralized decision making in Part 2.

Finally, decision making in the Predictable Success organization doesn't stop with the making of the decision itself. If anything, in Predictable Success the greater focus is on the *execution* of that decision once it is made. Once a decision has been made, it doesn't languish in limbo, with the managers hoping it will gain traction or acceptance—put simply, it just gets done. As we'll see, the main reason for this is that in Predictable Success decisions are not made by a closeted team of managers, then tossed "over the transom" for frontline employees to implement, but rather are made by involving *from the start* all those who will be materially impacted, thus achieving buy-in and momentum right from the get-go.

## 2. Goal Setting: The Ability to Readily Set and Consistently Achieve Goals.

The second characteristic of Predictable Success is the one that both Mike and Gloria had most obviously lost, though for different reasons: *the ability to readily set and consistently achieve their goals.*

When I speak with an executive whose organization has made it to Predictable Success, this is the one aspect of being there that he or she most values and refers to most frequently—getting back a sense of really being in control, being able to make things happen once more. As Jeffrey Immelt, CEO of GE, puts it: "When you put your foot on the gas in this company, the car goes forward."

> I refer here to the organization's internal ability to easily set and achieve their goals. No methodology can inure an organization against catastrophic **external** events such as a market collapse or demographic shifts, although, as we'll see, the Predictable Success organization will be consistently more nimble in responding to such external events.

Both Mike and Gloria had lost the ability to "make the car go forward." And as they both discovered, when this happens, the person in charge doesn't notice the effect for quite some time. Months, maybe even years can pass before it becomes clear that the goal-setting (and goal-achieving) process is broken.

After all, you're still the boss—you're still having budgets made, setting goals, agreeing to business plans. Your people do *respond* when goals and targets are set. "Things" are still happening—meetings are held, resource allocations are made, emails are sent, progress reports are written. But months later, in spite of all that activity, just like Mike and Gloria, you look up to see that nothing of note has actually happened—your organization has stalled, or worse, it is going backward. It seems as though nothing you do or say "moves the needle" anymore.

This sense of helplessness—the feeling that try as you might, nothing you do or say is translating into substantive on-the-ground progress—can be devastating. Most executives are task-focused, strong-minded individuals who've gotten where they are by "getting things done," so coming to a realization that the car won't go forward when they step on the gas is intensely frustrating for them.

In contrast, managers in Predictable Success organizations can feel a direct linkage between their metaphoric right foot (the gas pedal) and the organization's acceleration. The goal-setting process is accomplished with relative ease (I say "relative" because no goal-setting process is without some pain, but in the Predictable Success organization, it's radically reduced) and it *is* a process—not an event. Goal setting is part of the warp and woof of the Predictable Success organization; it happens seamlessly, as part of the day-to-day operation of the business, not as the resource-sucking, do-it-at-the-last-minute event that it is in so many other organizations. Once goals have been set, barring catastrophic external events, the organization then moves relentlessly toward the achievement of those goals.

That's not to say Predictable Success organizations don't sometimes miss their targets—of course they do—but they hit them more often than they miss them, and when it *does* look as though they will miss their goals, they know about it early and take timely, corrective action.

# 3. Alignment: Structure, Process and People Are in Harmony.

In most organizations, there are considerable efficiency losses caused by the interaction between the three main "moving parts" of the organization—its *structure*, its *processes* and the *people* who work within both. Put more simply, a lot of time and energy is expended by people because they have to manipulate the organization's processes and/or structure in order to get things done.

In the "upward" part of the growth cycle (Early Struggle, Fun and Whitewater), the processes and structure are typically underdeveloped, leaving the people in the organization to compensate by working out systems and policies on their own—in turn leading to duplication, inefficiency and increasingly frustrated customers. In the "downward" part of the growth cycle—from Treadmill on—the systems and structure are overdeveloped and increasingly rigidly enforced, draining from employees the ability to show initiative and be innovative.

In Predictable Success, the organization achieves balance between structure, process and people. There is just the right amount of process to ensure that things get done in a consistent and efficient way, and just the right amount of structure to provide the railroad tracks for the organization to run on. People have the optimum degree of autonomy and freedom necessary to keep the organization vibrant and innovative, but there are enough controls and systems to manage risk, avoid unnecessary duplication, and prevent the organization from becoming exposed or vulnerable to a few superstar Big Dogs (high performers who also have a monopoly of knowledge about how the organization works—we'll learn much more about Big Dogs later).

In Predictable Success the matrix of structure, process and people is *interconnected* and *organic*, not fixed and absolute. In the Predictable Success organization, there is a realization that what worked yesterday may not work today, and accordingly, the interplay between structure, process and people is constantly shifting, staying fluid to meet the organization's changing needs. Through the use of cross-functional teams, process improvement events, and the genuine empowerment of supervisors and team leaders, the organization's structure and processes are constantly changing and evolving, rather like a lava lamp (for those of you too young to know what a lava lamp is, Wikipedia is your friend).

# 4. Accountability: Employees Become Self-accountable, in Addition to Being Externally Accountable to others.

The single most powerful characteristic of the Predictable Success organization is the existence of a culture of *self-accountability*. In the Predictable Success organization, everyone from the senior management to the truck drivers, receptionists and janitors has a strong sense of self-accountability toward their own and their team's responsibilities.

Why is there such a strong commitment to self-accountability in Predictable Success? It comes directly from the decision-making culture we discussed in Point 1 above. When empowered to make decisions of genuine import about their own jobs and responsibilities—and given the resources and the freedom to do what it takes to implement those decisions (see Point 3 on structure, processes and people)—each employee personally buys in to the success of his or her own and the team's activities.

With this strong sense of accountability comes a commitment to genuine achievement (rather than checking boxes or putting in face time). In Predictable Success, there are fewer turf battles, and individuals or teams do not work in "silos," cut off from each other and working independently. Instead, groups and teams work harmoniously and cross-functionally, sharing knowledge and experiences, building a social network that supplements the more formalized organization structure. Information flows where it needs to, untrammeled by micromanagement or "information hoarders," as the teams and groups in the organization drive toward *results* rather than self-justification or personal glory.

A secondary result of this high degree of self-accountability is that there is little room for time wasters, pencil pushers or "politicians" in Predictable Success—and the organization becomes increasingly competent at exposing and expunging those who become "makeweight." Mediocrity, willful underperformance or simple shirking of responsibility stands out so clearly that the underperforming individual has few places to hide.

This culture of self-accountability in the Predictable Success organization doesn't come simply from wishful thinking—rather, all the organization's structure and process is focused on demanding and delivering it. From the hiring process, where self-accountability is identified as a must-have attitude, training and mentoring and coaching, and by being modeled by senior management, self-accountability is at the core of Predictable Success.

# 5. Ownership: Employees Take Personal Responsibility for Their Actions and Outcomes.

Most leaders of organizations (or divisions, departments, groups or teams) feel at some point as if they are pushing an increasingly large rock uphill—that if they don't constantly put their shoulder into it, the whole thing will begin to lose momentum and eventually start to run downhill, losing all the gains that have been painstakingly made so far. One of the reasons managers take few vacations, work long hours and sometime just plain burn out is just this—the fear that if they don't push and push and push some more, all the progress they have made in growing their business will be lost.

In Predictable Success the situation is reversed. The organization, possessing each of the characteristics above (the ability to readily make and consistently implement decisions; the ability to readily set, and consistently achieve goals; having structure, process and people in harmony; and with a culture of self-accountability at the core), reaches a whole new phase of organizational growth—one where its growth and development are achieved by *everyone taking ownership and pulling together,* rather than by the manager group constantly "pushing."

In Predictable Success, managers get to do what they do best—manage. Instead of firefighting and fixing things, compensating for the poor work of others, or simply doing things because "I can do it better than anyone else," the manager becomes what they were meant to be in the first place: an overseer, a resource allocator and an innovator, supporting, motivating and leading those on the front line.

In the Predictable Success organization, there is no dependency culture around the management team—instead, there is a deep sense of co-dependency: managers are dependent on their teams for delivering results, and the frontline employees are dependent on their managers for guidance, advice and leadership. One is as important as the other, and together, they "pull" the organization toward its growth goals.

## Time for Mike and Gloria to Take the First Step . . .

Mike drained his second espresso (we met in Starbucks this time), and I watched as he mentally processed what I had just shared with him. I'd explained the Predictable Success growth cycle, briefly describing each of the seven stages. From the data he'd collected for me and my notes from our meetings, I'd showed him why I felt he was in Whitewater. In fact, I hadn't had to explain my conclusions for too long: "Stop." He turned his palms outward. "You don't need to convince me anymore—the very word Whitewater says it all—that's exactly what we're going through."

Mike concentrated intently, taking occasional notes as I explained the silver lining—that although his business was shuddering right now, he was in fact very close to Predictable Success—just one "growth step" away. Slowly, I talked him through the five characteristics of a Predictable Success organization—decision making; setting and achieving goals;

structure, process and people in harmony; self-accountability; pull not push. There was no doubt: Mike was hooked. I could tell from his nods and his looks of recognition, from what he wrote down and what he didn't need to write, that Mike understood the power of getting his organization to Predictable Success. I had just one question: Was he ready to take the necessary steps to get there?

"Ready?" said Mike, setting down his cup. "I've never felt so ready to do anything in my entire life." He looked right into my eyes, and I knew what his next question would be. He smiled as he asked, "What do we do first?"

"First," I said, reaching for my schedule, "you and your team need to understand exactly why and how you got here. Only by knowing what causes Whitewater can you start the process of moving to the next step—to Predictable Success. When is your team free to meet?"

As we flicked our schedules back and forward, comparing dates, I noticed my upcoming meeting with Gloria. Persuading someone that their organization was in Treadmill was always a more difficult process than with someone in Whitewater. It was going to be an interesting meeting . . .

## SUMMARY

- Predictable Success is a natural stage in every organization's growth.
- In Predictable Success, the organization can easily set and consistently achieve its goals.
- Predictable Success is not about an organization's size, age or resources.
- Nor is Predictable Success a specific corporate culture, a way of having meetings or industry-specific.
- An organization must progress through the earlier stages of development to reach Predictable Success. It cannot jump a stage (though it can reduce the time spent there), but it can cycle through various stages.
- An organization can stay in Predictable Success indefinitely.
- An organization in Predictable Success benefits specifically from better decision making, goal setting, alignment, accountability and ownership.

# [ CHAPTER TWO ]

## EARLY STRUGGLE: GASPING FOR CASH, FINDING A MARKET—OVERCOMING GRAVITY TO ACHIEVE TAKEOFF

"The first road to freedom is viability."
—Rupert Murdoch

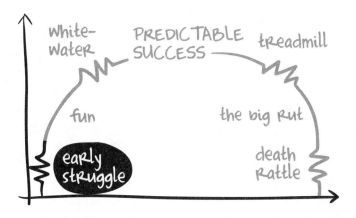

IT WAS A BLEAK BELFAST DAY, WITH RAIN SLATTING AGAINST THE windows. I was sitting in a well-appointed boardroom with my then-business partner, Ronnie. We sat side by side at the conference table, poring over spreadsheets. Both of us had been accountants in a prior life, so we had no excuse for not understanding what we were seeing: Our business was aborting on takeoff.

Two years earlier, Ronnie and I had formed a corporation to acquire a master license for the Pizza Hut franchise for Ireland, which committed us to opening ten restaurants in five years. Now, two years and four restaurants later, we were hemorrhaging cash. We had seriously underestimated the capital we needed to acquire leases and build the restaurants, and new construction had shuddered to a halt. If we didn't do something soon, the franchisor could pull our license, and everything we had accomplished so far would be lost.

As we pondered our options, I stood up and strolled to the large windows overlooking Belfast's bustling main street, still crowded in the rain (in Ireland, if you stayed in when it rained, you'd never go out). *So many people*, I thought—and yet, we only need a small percentage of them to eat in our restaurants. I knew this business wasn't complicated: Get enough people in the door, control your labor and food costs, and bingo—you have a profit. It was the simplicity and formulaic nature of the business that had attracted Ronnie and me to the Pizza Hut franchise in the first place.

So what had gone wrong? If the formula was so simple, why were we struggling to get off the ground?

Looking at the spreadsheets, the answer was pretty straightforward, and hardly original or unique to us. We were simply running out of the fuel we needed—cash—and on takeoff, no less.

## Overcoming Gravity

As I stared out the window, scenes unfolded in my mind from the past two years—Ronnie and I in board meetings, on construction sites, in lawyers' offices: fleeting images of the time, money and effort Ronnie and I had poured into trying to get this business off the ground. All that energy, all that effort—and yet we were going nowhere.

Then, from somewhere in my subconscious, another image came to mind. This one was from my childhood twenty years earlier, when as a rapt thirteen-year-old I had watched the five massive F1 engines of a Saturn V rocket lifting Apollo 11 into space. I couldn't help but smile as I thought of that image of sheer power, lifting the previously immobile, weighty rocket vertically upward, straining to escape the gravity of earth. Our mission was perhaps not as audacious as putting a man on the moon (although persuading people in Ireland to eat flat Italian bread instead of fish and chips was quite a challenge), but nonetheless, that image encapsulated what our problem was: We had seriously underestimated the resources we needed to get our business off the ground. We were trying to take off with one engine when we really needed five.

Over the next fifteen years, as I helped launch more than forty businesses, I would recall that image—of the sheer energy and power needed to lift Apollo 11 off the tarmac and into orbit—over and over again, until eventually it became indelibly linked in my mind with the process of launching any new venture. As I was to find out from extreme personal experience, the struggle Ronnie and I had in achieving "liftoff" with the Pizza Hut franchise was not unique. Far from it. Over time, I came to realize that what we experienced with Pizza Hut was simply one version of something that, to a greater or lesser extent, I would experience every time I launched a new business.

Eventually, I recognized a pattern: No matter how a new venture is launched, no matter what preparations you make or how much you think you've learned from "the last time," the first stage in every new venture is a fight to achieve liftoff. I gave it a name: Early Struggle.

I discovered that while Early Struggle is never exactly the same for each new venture, because every new business has its own unique set of variables—the skills, knowledge and experience of the founding entrepreneurs, how established the product and market is, and how much cash there is to start with, for example, I learned that while the intensity and duration of Early Struggle can vary greatly, one thing is sure: The stage itself is unavoidable. As I was to find out (and as you will see later in this book), just like every other stage on the road to Predictable Success, you can't detour past Early Struggle or skip over it—the only thing you can do is to minimize the time you spend there.

# What Early Struggle Is

Of all the stages in Predictable Success, the first, Early Struggle, is the easiest to define: It's a race to establish a viable market before the initial cash runs out.

For the founders of any new business, it often seems as though there are a lot of unknowns: location, name, color scheme, logo, hiring, buying, which phone carrier . . . These and a thousand other things, large and small, loom in the mist, demanding attention.

But the reality is that there are really only two unknowns that count:

1. Are there enough people out there who will buy your product or service at a profit?

2. Do you have enough fuel (cash) to pay the bills until you find them?

As figure 2.1 shows, Early Struggle is essentially a race against time to swap dependence on externally generated cash (capital funding) with cash generated from profitable trading:

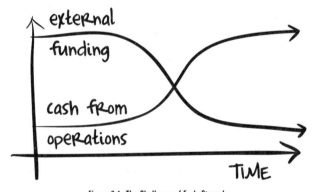

Figure 2.1: The Challenge of Early Struggle

Although it can vary considerably, for those businesses that successfully make it through Early Struggle, the phase generally lasts about three years, and looks something like this:

**Year 1:** Get up and running, work out the operational details and establish a supply chain.

**Year 2:** Prove the market, obtain a consistent flow of customers and get the pricing structure right.

**Year 3:** Gain sustained traction in the marketplace, and generate operational cash inflows that exceed outflows on a regular basis.

As you can readily deduce, there are three main variables that determine how long Early Struggle will last for your new venture: (1) how easily you can access external funding; (2) how quickly you can find a viable market for your product or service; and (3) how effective you are in using (1) to get you to (2). We'll look at each of these in more detail a little later.

# The Unique Danger in Early Struggle

Before we examine strategies for coping with and (more important) getting out of Early Struggle, we need to first look at a unique feature of this phase—a dark side, if you will, that sets Early Struggle aside and apart from every other stage in Predictable Success.

Along with the simplicity of its challenge—get to a viable market before the money runs out—Early Struggle brings with it an equally simple but stark consequence: If your businesses fails in this, it will die.

The reason is pretty straightforward: There is no other option.

As you'll see later, if a business hits problems in any other stage of Predictable Success, it can always retrace its steps back to an earlier stage in development, regroup and prepare for another push. However, unlike the later stages on the path to Predictable Success, in Early Struggle there are no previous stages—so there's nowhere to go backward to. Only by facing—and overcoming—the challenge of Early Struggle can a new venture survive, move forward to its next stage of development and advance toward Predictable Success. The option to return to an earlier stage and regroup does not exist. The option is binary: up or out.

For this reason, for most new ventures, Early Struggle is the most dangerous time they will face, and it is not surprising that, as a consequence the rate of "infant mortality" in new ventures is very high. Many more businesses die than make it through Early Struggle.

If you examine the official data in most developed countries (for example, from the Internal Revenue Service in the US, or from Customs and Excise or the Inland Revenue in the UK), the numbers are pretty consistent: About two-thirds of all registered businesses don't survive past the first three years. As any practicing CPA will tell you, the actual figure is much higher: Because many businesses never make it to the stage where they register with their local authorities, their statistics aren't even on record. By many people's estimates, including my own, a truer estimate is that about 80 percent of all new ventures never make it through Early Struggle.

So the unique danger of Early Struggle is simple—the chances are high of not making it out the other end. If you do make it through Early Struggle, that's all that's required. It doesn't have to be pretty, it just has to happen. But if you don't make it through Early Struggle, it's over—there's nothing else to do but to shut up shop and, if you're brave, try again another time.

## Strategies for Dealing with Early Struggle

From the previous section you should by now recognize that you can have only one strategy when in Early Struggle: to get out of it as quickly as possible.

Although (as we'll see) there are plausible reasons why you might dawdle in some of the other stages on your way to Predictable Success, in Early Struggle your sole aim must be to pass through as rapidly as possible and move on to the next stage. There are too many dangers, and the rate of infant mortality is too high, to hang around in Early Struggle.

Put it this way: You don't want to have a strategy for *dealing with* Early Struggle—you want a strategy for *getting out of* Early Struggle. Which begs an important point: *Beware of becoming involved with people who are addicted to Early Struggle.*

This might sound crazy, but believe it or not, there are people out there who are addicted to the Early Struggle phase and are constitutionally incapable of getting themselves out of it. I know—I've been involved with more than a few, and it's both expensive (in time, money and energy) and ultimately futile.

Now, I'm not talking here about serial entrepreneurs. True entrepreneurs have a healthy respect for Early Struggle, and some are prepared to take it on multiple times as part of the price they pay to launch a new business—they may go back into Early Struggle frequently, but they do so with the stated goal of getting through it as soon as possible and out the other side.

I'm talking instead about people who, for various reasons, become addicted to being in Early Struggle, and who want to stay there indefinitely: maybe they love playing the venture capital game, or they get hooked on the crazy start-up vibe, or they adore their patented gizmo so much that they can't bear actually commercializing it. Whatever their reason, if you're not careful they will suck you in, trap you with them in Early Struggle, drain all your resources, then move on to the next willing partner.

Here are the three key distinctions that will help you tell if you're hooking up with a true entrepreneur or an ESO (Early Struggle Obsessive):

1. An ESO revels in the experience—"What a cool office this guy has. Can we visit with him another time?" An entrepreneur is focused on results—"Did we get the money?"

2. An ESO is rigidly unrealistic—"It's got to be made of platinum. I designed it in platinum, and that's what it's got to be." An entrepreneur is passionate but flexible—"This company will place an order for 5,000 in plastic. I vote plastic."

3. An ESO sabotages success—"She thinks she's so smart. I can't work with her. Get her out of here." An entrepreneur craves it "She's smart and effective at selling our product. She's staying."

Do yourself a favor and stay away from Early Struggle Obsessives.

# How to Get Out of Early Struggle

As we've seen, in Early Struggle your key goal is simple—get out of it, as fast as possible.

Earlier, we briefly identified the three key steps to getting out of Early Struggle. Let's look at them now in more detail:

## 1. MAXIMIZE YOUR ACCESS TO EXTERNAL FUNDING.

My rule of thumb for years has been this: Whatever your business plan says you need, triple it.

It's a simple formula, and guess what? It works. I don't mean that it's by any means simple—raising money never is, and raising three times your original estimate may well take more than three times the effort—but if you can do it, it works. Get what you can, from wherever you can, then get some more.

Now that doesn't mean "giving away the shop" on day one: I'm not proposing that you trade equity for cash in every circumstance. But I do mean that if you have the opportunity to get hold of cash on reasonable terms, take it. If you end up with too much, you can always give some of it back.

A quick word about "bootstrapping": What if you're launching your business on a wing and a prayer, using your credit cards, keeping things tight, starting small and allowing the business to grow without recourse to "traditional" external sources of capital? Well, two things:

First of all, it's a great way to launch a business—I've done it myself more often than not; and secondly, the same rule applies: However much you estimated you'd need to cash in on your credit cards or your 401(k), or fund from sales, triple it. Then breathe deeply, grab the bootstraps tighter, and go out there and get it. If that means grabbing someone else's bootstraps as well, by way of partnership, think seriously about doing it.

When you're struggling to find any money at all to launch your new venture, it may sound glib, even flip, to hear me casually say, "Triple it"—certainly when I was launching my first businesses thirty years ago, I would have sneered at such a suggestion. But forty-plus start-ups later, I know what I'm going up against in Early Struggle—and I know what's needed to come out the other side.

Remember that statistic on failure during Early Struggle—80 percent. Many of those businesses failed simply because they were underfunded to begin with.

## 2. MINIMIZE THE PATH TO A VIABLE MARKET.

One of the most important reasons for securing ready access to external funding is simply so that you can focus on something much more important: finding a viable market.

Believe it or not, a lot of businesses never make it out of Early Struggle because they concentrate too much on raising capital. It's important to remember that while raising external cash is a good and important exercise, it's not your ultimate goal—your ultimate goal is viability—and in Early Struggle that means focusing laserlike on finding a viable market for your goods and services.

Practically speaking, this means doing four things:

**Prioritize.** Getting closer to finding (and gaining traction with) a profitable market for your product or service should be your number one priority at all times. Everything else is secondary. You must have a mechanism—a meeting, if you must, but more likely an email, a Post-it or a foghorn—to remind everyone, every day, of your absolute commitment to finding a market and becoming viable. You should finish every day by answering this question: "What did we do today that took us closer to finding a viable market for our product (or service)?"

**Listen.** For some reason I've never been able to quite fathom, the vast majority of new businesses jump into life in fully formed "transmit" mode. They barge into the marketplace like a boorish first date, talking incessantly about themselves, who they are, what they do and their value proposition, barely taking a breath, certainly never asking questions about the pretty girl opposite. Unless you're heavily into rejection, don't do that.

Plan to start your business in "listen" mode—you'll find out where your customers are by asking, not by talking.

**Experiment.** So your business plan says you'll make 5,000 Widgets in blue, and 3,000 Blodgetts in green. After listening to the marketplace, you might want to try offering 500 Blodgetts in pink. Or 250 Widgets unpainted in a "paint your own Widget" promo. Who knows? The market knows, not you.

And the only way you'll find out what they want is through experimentation. (This has been one of the greatest recent developments in the world of start-ups—with the rise of pay-per-click advertising and social media, experimentation in the marketplace is available at a scale and cost unimaginable even five years ago.)

**Adapt.** Hubris is a killer in Early Struggle. Accept this, and you will get to viability much quicker: Your business plan is wrong. Your mission statement is wrong. In all likelihood, even what you think are your core values are wrong. Not because you're dumb, but because you created them in a vacuum. Now that you're out in the dynamic, changing, real world, your business plan, your mission statement, maybe even some of your values will need to change to survive.

## 3. CONNECT YOUR FUNDING TO YOUR MARKET IN AS SHORT A DISTANCE AS POSSIBLE.

Remember the sainted dotcom era? If so, you'll recall that a lot of businesses with a lot of cash went kaput very quickly—because they didn't effectively use that cash to attain their ultimate goal of finding a viable market. Perhaps you remember computer.com? I thought not. This company spent $2.6 million dollars—60 percent of its entire capital—on one Super Bowl ad. One. Super Bowl. Ad. It then promptly went bust.

Now, that era of conspicuous maltreatment of otherwise perfectly good money may have passed, but the same mistake still occurs in many (I would say, on the basis of my own experience, most) new ventures: not being smart about how to spend capital to gain market. Here are the most egregious errors to avoid:

**Fancy offices and custom-designed work environments.** You might not be emulating the dotcom era with twelve conference rooms furnished with cherrywood tables and Aeron chairs, but until you secure your market, invest in "cheap and cheerful." Think IKEA rather than Herman Miller.

**Consultant fees.** Even aside from the expense of retaining consultants, Early Struggle is no time to let anyone—however strong their brand name is—get between you and your intended market. Whether it's focus groups, product testing or market research, do it yourself. Remember the importance of listening? Don't delegate it.

**Branding.** You're not going to get your branding right at the beginning, so don't spend money as if you have. Design and branding can and should evolve as you get closer to your market and you hear the marketplace chatter more and more clearly. Don't spend to have a brand spring fully formed on day one as if you know exactly what your customer will want. Apart from being expensive, it's counterproductive.

Throughout Early Struggle, keep your ultimate goal in the forefront of your mind at all times: Every dollar you spend should take you a step closer to finding a viable market for your product or service.

Got your start-up funding? Check. Focused on finding a viable market? Check. Being smart about using your funding to find your market? Check.

Cool . . . then it's time to get out of Early Struggle and go have some Fun.

## SUMMARY

- Early Struggle is the first stage of every organization's development.
- During Early Struggle, the main challenge is reaching financial stability before the founder's resources (time and energy) run out.
- As many as 80 percent of new ventures never make it through Early Struggle.
- To get through Early Struggle, founders must find a viable market as soon as possible and use their start-up funding wisely.
- It is fatal to get distracted in Early Struggle and to lose focus on the main goal—to get out of Early Struggle and into the next stage of development: Fun.

# ⟦ CHAPTER THREE ⟧

## FUN: SELL, SELL, SELL—FAST GROWTH
## AND EARLY SUCCESS

"I want to run a company where we are moving too quickly and trying too much. If we don't
[make] any mistakes, we're not taking enough risk."
—Larry Page, Google cofounder

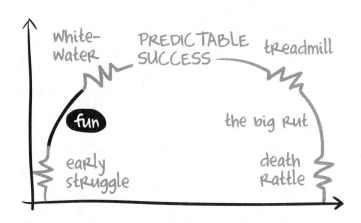

AS THE TWIN-ENGINE LIGHT AIRCRAFT BANKED DOWN OVER THE
treetops and steadied out, ready for touchdown, I looked up from the
reports I was only vaguely reading and tried to remember where I was
flying to. Let's see—retracing my steps would be easiest . . . Left from

Belfast . . . two days in London . . . on to our office in San Francisco . . . back up to visit our affiliate in Toronto . . . then . . . ? I looked out the window—forests, a beautiful river . . . ah yes, I remembered: The plane was descending into the pretty capital of one of Canada's maritime provinces.

This disorientation had gotten to be a common experience in recent months—having to look at boarding passes to recall which flight was next, writing room numbers on the palm of my hand (those plastic key cards being resolutely mute on the matter). And time zones—always, eternally calculating time zones: who was awake where, in our various offices—who could I call without getting them out of bed in the middle of the night, who would be expecting me to check in about now, who was about to start work, who was finishing for the day? My two-time-zone watch always seemed about three time zones shy of the information I needed.

This leg of the trip was to be a short one—just two days in which I would be hooking up with my business partner to meet with state government officials to discuss our entrepreneurship development program. A couple of years earlier, the two of us had gotten together to train entrepreneurs in launching and growing new businesses, and our new venture had taken off like wildfire. Local government agencies couldn't get enough of what we were offering (building indigenous businesses being a highly desirable thing for any local economy), and within eighteen months the success of our early programs had rocketed us out of Early Struggle.

## Time for a "Board Meeting"

Now it seemed we couldn't find enough hours in the day to respond to everyone who wanted to know about our programs. Add to that the swift pace at which our company was growing to manage the work we had already undertaken. My partner and I were pretty much in a constant state of giddy excitement. Stressful, overworked, overscheduled, overstretched excitement, but excitement nonetheless.

Part of the excitement came from the very reason we had flown here to Canada's eastern extremity. Word of the success of our programs had made it to some economic development officers within local government agencies here, and we'd been asked if we would come and talk to them about how we might help their state by developing an entrepreneurship program locally. It was typical of the kind of unsolicited calls we were getting out of the blue on an almost daily basis from potential clients— can we come see them, or failing that, can they come see us? It seemed as though business was falling from the sky, and in order to respond to it all, my partner and I usually split the sales visits between us. This was to be one of those rare occasions when we would be meeting up to spend a little time together: It wasn't that we both needed to be there for the sales pitch, it was just that this was the only way we could get face time together. And hey, for two young(ish) guys full of energy and enthusiasm, what was flying halfway round the world for a brief meeting, anyway? We called these frequent though brief, halfway-round-the-world meet-ups our "board meetings." We were having fun.

As it turned out, this leg of our trip was a bust, even if it was a fun bust: At our first meeting, held just an hour after I had landed, we discovered that the people who had contacted us actually represented three different local development agencies. And it soon became very clear to my partner and me that while each agency really, really wanted us to come and set up a version of our program in its region, it also really, really wanted the other agencies to pay for it. Nobody was willing to reach into their own budget and make a commitment to pay our fees. They also made it clear that this situation was unlikely to change in that budgetary year, as all three agencies were pretty much tapped out. Bummer.

## Onward!

No problemo. No holding back our intrepid heroes! We regrouped over a cup of coffee in our hotel lobby and in short order decided that the meetings we'd slated for that afternoon and the next day—to discuss the details of a program that clearly was never going to happen—would be a waste of everyone's time. A couple of calls later, our assistant had rescheduled our flights to get us out of town and on our way that evening. As we explained to a confused desk clerk that we wouldn't be needing the rooms that we hadn't yet checked in for, a car arrived to take us and our unpacked bags back to the same airport we'd arrived at just hours earlier that morning. Onward!

I was heading to Singapore, where I had precisely three days to find and staff a local office ahead of a major client's visit, and my partner was flying to Sydney, Australia, to look at the possibilities of us doing business there and in New Zealand. We arranged to meet for our next "board meeting" one week later in Hong Kong—after all, it was perfectly positioned at the intersection of our itineraries, and no doubt the Mandarin Oriental could supply us with a suitable meeting room.

We weren't just having fun . . . we were having Fun—with a capital "F."

## What Fun Is

After Early Struggle, Fun is the second stage in any organization's development. It is typically characterized by fast, early-stage growth, frantic (if not frenzied) focus on acquiring and satisfying customers, and an underlying sense of, well . . . fun.

The reason for the "fun" part is threefold: First, just getting out of Early Struggle is in itself a reason to celebrate. After all that grinding to survive, who wouldn't want to have a little fun? Second, at this point in its development, the business is acquiring new customers fast (we'll see why shortly)—and for any entrepreneur, that really *is* fun. Third, there's finally some money to spare. After all that penny-pinching, we're finally making money, and spending it (even just some of it) is fun!

Compared to the inward-looking tenseness of Early Struggle ("Will we survive? Will we hold on long enough?"), in Fun there is more of a feeling of outward-looking ease ("Hey, we made it! And look at all this new business lying around!"). There's positive momentum and energy, and less of a sense of pushing a large rock uphill.

Emerging from Early Struggle unleashes a lot of latent energy: With cash flow stabilized and the market identified, the founder/owners are reinvigorated, their sense of excitement is renewed, and their confidence, dented by the pain of Early Struggle, returns to its previously high level. With that sense of release—almost like being let off a leash—the business accelerates out of Early Struggle into Fun, with a tight, centralized team (usually based around the founder/owners) producing fast, customer-driven growth.

In Fun, the chief focus of the business shifts from stabilizing cash flow and finding a market to selling, pure and simple. It's not that cash flow becomes unimportant—it's simply that in Fun, the business is making sales at such a rate, and has such relatively low costs, that the cash flow seems to look after itself.

As for finding a market—the market has been identified during Early Struggle, so in Fun, the focus is all about *mining* the market. The newly energized organization seemingly can't help but find customers and converts, and the business grows rapidly: Fun is almost always accompanied by fast, customer-led growth. We've seen some of the reasons already—unleashed energy, positive cash flow and clarity about the market—but the other major contributing factor is simple statistics: The organization's market share is so small (usually close to zero at the beginning of Fun) that double-digit growth is easily attainable.

## Managing an Organization That's in Fun

Fun businesses are usually (though not always) managed by the owner(s). Because it is only the second stage of development, right after Early Struggle, usually the original founders are still in charge. Because of the organization's young age and relative simplicity, the organization structure is simple. It usually looks like something I call the "Sun and Moons":

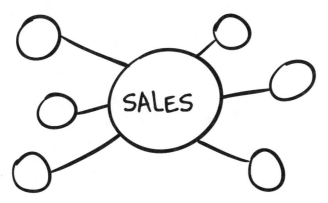

Figure 3.1 Organization Structure During Fun

As you can see, everything in the organization is focused on one thing—sales. The sales function is primary, and everything else is a satellite activity with just one goal: to do anything and everything that the sales function desires or needs (as we'll see later, that distinction—between what sales desires and what it needs, will become a crucial one). Management, such as it is, is hands-on and heavily sales- and operations-focused, with the owners actively involved in every major decision and activity.

Management decisions are usually about flexibility and responsiveness: How fast can we get this proposal out? When will that product arrive? How can we fix this problem quickly and get on to the next thing? There is a high degree of transparency throughout the young organization, and the small, loyal team can be depended on to go the extra mile when needed—which is often. Decision making is highly centralized, flowing out from the founder/owners; job titles are fluid, and management expects everyone to pitch in and do whatever is necessary to please the customer (or the sales force).

# The Rise of the Big Dogs

As we've seen, the primary focus of the organization during Fun is on customer acquisition—obtaining sales. As a direct consequence, high-performing salespeople become the "superstars" of the organization. As our organization chart (Figure 3.1) shows, the sales function (and hence the salespeople) are the center of the Fun organization's solar system. All other functions—however important to ultimate customer satisfaction—are subordinate, whether it be design, engineering, purchasing, installation, service, admin or warehousing. Sales comes first.

During this stage, phrases such as "The customer is king" and "Everything starts with a sale—all else follows" become mantras. Sales is all; everything else is secondary. The employees who work in the other (non-sales) functions, however skilled they may be, rarely will have the same degree of access, political power or influence as the Big Dogs in sales.

This primacy of the sales function during Fun is not abnormal or unreasonable—it is as it should be during this stage in the organization's life cycle. During Fun, revenue from sales is like air to a mammal—without it, the organization cannot survive. In later developmental stages, the organization can afford to shift the focus from sales for a while and still survive (and, as we'll see, will actually need to do so). But when in Fun, the organization has too thin an asset base to survive should it take its eye off selling for even a short time.

There are many excellent small businesses that make it out of Early Struggle but that eschew sales-based growth, preferring instead to focus primarily on their craft—be it graphic design, software development or car repair. For these master craftspeople, business growth is consciously sublimated to producing quality product for a few loyal customers. These are often superlative businesses to deal with—I use many of them myself—but their organizational development is limited (they usually move back and forth between Early Struggle and early Fun), and thus they are not the subject of this book.

Consequently, it's not surprising that during Fun those salespeople who consistently deliver growing sales revenues, month in and month out, rise to the status of Big Dogs. The owner/manager(s) may well be Big Dogs themselves—entrepreneurs are often, though not always, superb salespeople—but at the very least the owner/manager(s) will intuitively recognize the vital importance of good salespeople if their business is to stay alive and grow during Fun. As a result, over time the Big Dogs increasingly move to the center of the organization's power base: They have the ready ear of the boss because they're in contact several times a day, discussing potential new business and existing deals; they are a natural source of advice and opinion should the owner/manager(s) want it; they control the lifeblood of the organization (revenue); and they are typically loyal and hard-working to a fault.

The biggest of the Big Dogs can become so central to the success of the business that they develop "sweat equity." This happens when a Big Dog contributes so much to the early survival and success of the business that the owner group recognizes the Big Dog as having an informal, metaphorical investment in the business—of "sweat" rather than money. Later, we'll see that this sweat equity will need to be repaid, by either bonuses, real equity or, as happens most often, loyalty to the Big Dog in the face of difficulties later in the organization's development.

Although the rise of the Big Dogs in the sales function during Fun is both natural and vital for the growth of the business, as we'll see in the next chapter, it brings with it an inescapable future barrier to growth that will begin to appear as the organization matures and the Fun stage begins to transform into Whitewater.

## The Growth of Myths and Legends

Moving from Early Struggle to Fun unleashes entrepreneurial energies in a way that is unequaled at any later point in the organization's development—to continue the NASA space launch analogy from the previous chapter, this is the point at which the first-stage rockets fall away and the booster rockets propel the vehicle outside the Earth's gravitational pull. An enormous new forward momentum, which was held back and in a sense frustrated during Early Struggle, propels the organization into Fun.

Almost all of this explosive energy is directed toward acquiring and satisfying new customers. And as we've seen, finding new customers will never be easier than at this time in the organization's development. In fact, during the initial stages of Fun the tendency is to take on more business than the organization can reasonably deal with. No sale is turned away, no customization is too hard, no delivery deadline cannot be met: "Whatever the potential new customer wants, we'll promise it to them. We'll take on just about any job that's offered to us. In fact, strike that just about: We'll take on *any* job that's offered to us."

The reason for this lack of selectivity is threefold:

- The company is not yet confident that its market is truly sustainable; it fears these sales may be ephemeral and might disappear at any moment.
- The company has a thin asset base and is desperate to add to it with any revenues it can find.

- The company doesn't know its own boundaries or capabilities yet, so how does it know whether or not it can achieve something unless it tries?

But of course, every good entrepreneur has a highly attuned internal processing system, and what generally happens is that the seemingly "impossible" deadlines and customizations are indeed met, albeit after caffeine-enhanced all-nighters and hair-raising last-minute improvisations. If Customer A has been told it will receive its product on Tuesday, it's at the delivery dock at 5:00 p.m. on Tuesday—or maybe 5:01 p.m., but it's there, nonetheless. If Customer B wanted its Blodgetts in pink instead of the standard blue, it gets them in pink, even if the owner and the person who made the sale spent the entire night repainting the Blodgetts themselves.

It's understandable that these stories of bravado are remembered, repeated and celebrated. Over time, tales of snatching orders from competitors with audacious promises, fulfilling those promises, then providing outrageous customer service are subconsciously—sometimes consciously—transmuted into perceived norms. The outlandishly exceptional performance that is made possible by the huge energy unleashed in Fun (and facilitated by the young organization's transparent, flexible, turn-on-a-dime, lightweight organization structure) becomes a touchstone for future expectations.

As we'll see later, to reach Predictable Success, the distinction between these events as myths and legends—to be remembered and celebrated—and as operational norms—to be replicated—will become an important one.

# Working for an Organization in Fun

When an organization is in Fun, the pace is frantic, everyone is committed and (usually) morale is sky-high. While there will be fraught times, the close-knit team members—usually hired personally by the owner(s) and selected for their loyalty and positive attitude more than their skill set—is more often pulled closer by hard work and challenges than driven apart.

The Sun and Moons shape of the business is less like an organization chart (businesses in Fun rarely have operational titles, let alone an organization chart) than an acceptance of fact: "We need to make sales to survive and grow, and we're all here to either do that or help others do that."

Excitement comes from never knowing quite what the owner/manager group will do next, particularly during the middle and later stages of Fun when the seemingly unending success of early Fun builds self-confidence and risk taking to a frighteningly high level. Monday morning might bring an all-staff meeting to say we're about to start an Internet division, or open an office in Burundi, or start a partnership with a multinational competitor. Growth is everything, and the owners seem to be fascinated by putting pins on maps—more offices, more locations, more products, more services, more alignments, more variety, more, more, more . . .

Individuals who need a lot of structure, who desire titles and clear boundaries, or who thrive on process and systemization will become immensely frustrated working for an organization in Fun: Much of the fun of Fun is the high degree of personal challenge resulting from the unstructured, freewheeling, almost chaotic flexibility of the organization. Job responsibilities are rarely defined and rarely stay the same. Initiative is valued, projects morph constantly from one thing to another, and opportunities to do new things abound. The ability to cope with ambiguity and imprecision is vital. If you have that, Fun will indeed be fun.

This is not to say there aren't frustrations in working for an organization in Fun—there are many, and they almost all emanate from the owner/managers: the constant uncertainty about what will happen next; the inability to set one course and stick to it; the frequent 180-degree changes in direction; the unpredictable, seemingly capricious attitudes toward things like salary levels (set on a one-by-one basis with no overall structure), time off (no policy—just make your case, one situation at a time) and working hours (basically, you need to be there when they are, which is highly unpredictable). Together, it can be more than wearing. However the rewards are high—if not in a monetary sense, at least in getting to see how all aspects of a business work, and in being closer to the seat of power than is possible in any of the later stages in the organization's development.

# The Dangers of Fun

Doesn't sound as though much could go wrong in Fun, does it? After all, Fun is fun—where could the dangers lie? Well, just as happens if you leave unsupervised children to play by themselves, sooner or later something will go wrong. Here are the most common examples:

**1. The overfunded start-up that thinks it's in Fun but isn't.** You wouldn't think it was possible to "overfund" a start-up—after all, isn't our second principle of successful start-ups to get all the resources you need in order to find your viable, sustainable market? And didn't we say that whatever figure you thought of, you should triple it?

All true, but even so, it is possible (and not uncommon in the world of venture capital) to overfund a start-up to such an extent that the founders think and act as if they are in Fun, when in fact they are still in Early Struggle. From the outside—and eventually, because of the power of auto-suggestion, on the inside—the business looks and feels (and spends) as though it has a viable market, when really it should be focused on finding its market. Net result? The founders, desperate for more cash to keep the business afloat, redefine their market two or three times, each time convincing their investors to re-up, until eventually it dawns on those providing the money that this business isn't really viable at all, and they turn off the spigot.

**2. Out of control costs.** It's easy to get carried away in Fun and end up with a spiraling cost base that can drag the whole company under. Partially in reaction to the months (maybe years) of austerity in Early Struggle, and partially because of growing self-confidence as the company notches success after success, the founders add staff, then new offices in new locations, extravagant marketing campaigns and high levels of discretionary spending.

The net result is that one day the owners realize to their shock that the business is considerably in debt. Their initial reaction is "How can that be? We're selling so much, we couldn't be in debt." But of course what's happening is that the profits from the sales are no longer enough to fund the business's extravagant overheads.

The key to avoiding this is mundane: Invest in quality, timely accounting reports—and read them. Specifically, to maximize your Fun, invest ahead of the curve in cost accounting—breaking down your revenues and associated costs by project or customer, so that you know early on which jobs are profitable and which are not. Do this as early as possible—as soon as you've got your second customer, even though it will feel like overkill—and get used to reviewing your variable costs on every job and your fixed costs every month.

**3. Egomania.** All too often—particularly in the later stages of Fun, after sequential early successes have been achieved—the founders develop an Icarus complex and believe they can achieve almost anything they set their hands to. Eventually, they fly too close to the sun: an expansion too far, an office too many, a new product line that tanks, a joint venture that goes sour—a big ego can come in many guises, but eventually it ends in tears.

In my own experience, this can be either made worse or minimized depending on the choice of business partner. There is no worse chemistry for headstrong risk taking than pairing two highly competitive entrepreneurs as founders in the same venture. While they will enjoy the ride (and everyone else will enjoy watching it), eventually they'll egg each other into taking that one flight too close to the sun.

Conversely, a wisely chosen partnership of an outgoing entrepreneur and a feet-on-the-ground realist can do a lot to mitigate excessive and foolish risk taking (or unnecessary frippery, which, while less dramatic, can still add up to a weight the business cannot take). If you're an entrepreneur who doesn't have or want such a partnership, then do yourself a favor and get one or two people whose judgment you trust, and ask them to serve as informal advisors. You don't need to pay them or put them on the board—just go talk to them over coffee once a month. Tell them what you're up to and what you're planning, and listen to what they have to say. There's no guarantee that doing so will protect you from your own ego, but it reduces the likelihood that you'll do something entirely egregious.

# How to Get Out of Fun

The first question about getting out of Fun is "Why would you want to?" Who would want to move beyond a stage in business so exciting, so varied, and so challenging as Fun? The secret is in the name: Who would want to stop having . . . well, fun?

The answer is twofold: First of all, there are many, many people who don't. Their business is in Fun, they're *having* fun and that's where they intend to stay. Many excellent mom-and-pop businesses are in Fun and work hard to stay right there. Your favorite local deli or muffler shop or graphic designer probably is in the Fun stage, and that's one of the reasons it's your favorite—the business is in Fun, and that makes it fun to deal with.

In Fun, life can be good—sometimes very, very good. Fun is the stage in a businesse's development when a highly effective owner/manager can generate higher-than-average profitability and produce strongly positive cash flow. Fun is often when the owner/manager can begin to afford that second home, the boat, the golf club memberships, the foreign travel. Owning a business in the middle or later stages of Fun is like being a king in your own domain—you have a lot of power, and the rewards can be high.

Having had that experience, many business owners who have subsequently taken their business beyond Fun into one or more of the later stages in development have discovered that they either didn't like it there (e.g., when they made it into Whitewater or Treadmill) or weren't prepared to pay the price to stay there (e.g., in Predictable Success). Those same owners often make a conscious decision to retrace their steps—to downsize their business, if you will—to return to the Fun stage (even if that is not a phrase they would use).

Maybe you've seen a business—a local carpet store or restaurant, perhaps—expand to two, then three, then five or six locations, before the owners, harassed and unhappy, decide that they were much happier when they had just one or two stores, and take steps to get back to those halcyon days. Though they may never see it in such formal terms, that's a conscious decision to return to, and stay, in Fun.

Then there's everyone else: those owners who don't want to cap the growth of their business, who want to continue to grow as much as the market will allow. They may have very big ambitions or not-so-big ambitions, but either way their desire is to grow, not to run in place. For such owners, a strange dynamic takes over, and it's this:

They need not (and, mostly, will not) try to get out of Fun—instead, they will be "kicked out" of Fun automatically, as a consequence of growth.

Let me explain: For the managers of a growing business, there is no perceived need to "get out of Fun." At this point in their experience, few owners or managers even think in such terms. Even if they studied the concept of organizational life cycles in business school, they don't think of the growth of *their* business as moving from one stage of organizational development to another. It's like fish in water: Just as a fish doesn't know it's in something called "water" (it's just swimming around), few owners or managers are aware that they're in something called "Fun"—they're just going about their everyday business of running the company.

So to most owners and managers at this stage in development, growing the business is simply a matter of doing more of the same: "Let's do what we did yesterday, except let's do more of it." Growth is at this point merely a form of arithmetic—one plus one equals two, and we want more than two, so let's keep adding until we reach ten or one hundred, or one thousand or whatever our goal is. Growth feels as though it is an organic, natural process.

And for a while—early in Fun—it is. Until, unavoidably, growth brings with it one other thing—complexity. The simple, transparent, turn-on-a-dime business that employed only ten people in the early days of Fun grows, first to twenty-five, then fifty, then one hundred people. Now there are layers of management. Communication slows down. Inaccuracies begin to happen. The boss can no longer see—let alone instantly fix—everything that is happening. And one day, the unthinkable happens:

A customer is let down.

And at that point, everything begins—very slowly—to feel different. Gently at first, but discernibly, instead of the relatively smooth sailing that has been Fun so far, the business begins to rock a little from side to side. More things begin to go wrong. More mistakes are made. People begin to grab the sides. Profits slide. Water starts to lap over into the boat. And before you know it, without even trying, you've been kicked out of Fun.

Like it or not, you've just hit Whitewater.

## SUMMARY

- Fun is the second, natural step in every organization's development (assuming it survives Early Struggle).
- The main focus of the business in Fun is generating sales revenue.
- This leads to the rise of "Big Dogs"—those (often salespeople) who build sweat equity by contributing to the survival and growth of the business.
- During Fun, the organization builds "myths and legends" that will later become unrealistic performance expectations.
- Working for an organization in Fun is exciting, but requires the ability to cope with ambiguity.
- Sometimes, being in Fun can lead to overconfidence, which at its worst can cause the owners to take risks that maim or destroy the business.
- It is vital to monitor costs during Fun.
- Some owners choose never to leave Fun, because of the high rewards and, well, it's fun!
- After growing bigger, some people bring their business back to Fun because they like it there.
- If you continue to grow your business, you will be kicked out of Fun—into Whitewater—automatically.

# [ CHAPTER FOUR ]

## WHITEWATER: WHY ISN'T THIS FUN ANYMORE?
## BATTLING COMPLEXITY TO BECOME EFFICIENT

"You found a company, you run it, then it runs you."
—David Neeleman, former CEO of JetBlue

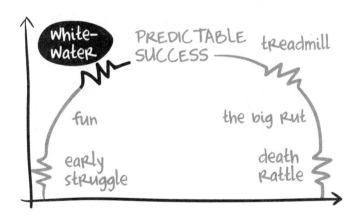

THE NUMBER ON THE CALLER ID SEEMED FAMILIAR, AND YET I couldn't place it precisely. The 415 area code put it somewhere in the San Francisco Bay Area, and as I'd lived there for four years, it was certainly possible that whoever was calling was someone I might know. So when

I picked up the phone I was surprised, but not shocked, to hear Robyn's voice—we had worked together two years previously, when her fast-growing graphic design agency was rocketing through Fun.

"Robyn! Great to hear from you. How are things in Sausalito?"

I'd meant the words as no more than the usual small talk at the beginning of any telephone conversation, but it was obvious from Robyn's sigh and long pause that to her, my casual question was not so casual—it was in fact the very reason she was calling me.

"Exhausting. Things here in Sausalito are exhausting," she said eventually. Her voice sounded thin and tired. "That's why I'm calling you."

I thought back to when I'd last pulled out of the parking lot of Robyn's offices, two years previously. I remembered looking back at the stunning view of San Francisco Bay, a corner of the Golden Gate Bridge visible through the trees in the beautifully manicured waterfront office park. I'd always liked coming here to work with Robyn—she and her team were as energizing and as creative and impressive as the surroundings they worked in. Their agency was an exciting, fun place to go, and helping her build a strategy for further growth had been an enjoyable learning experience for me—a true partnership with an exceptional team.

I smiled as I remembered Robyn's last words as I was leaving. Stooping down to my car window, she'd said: "You're right, Les—we're having fun, and I intend to keep it that way as long as I possibly can." She'd sent me on my way with a jovial bang on the car roof and a bright smile.

It didn't sound as though she was having much fun right now. "It's as if we've walked into quicksand," said Robyn. "Remember when you were here, how agile and flexible we were? Never left a client hanging? Never missed a deadline? That's all gone."

"Really?"

"Well, maybe not all gone . . . but . . . sheesh . . . very, very infrequent. These days, it's as though we're always coming from behind—always running to catch up." Robyn paused. "Les, I haven't been out to see a client personally for months. I'm constantly in meetings. Firefighting. Arguing with people." She paused again. "We never used to argue. Now Todd and Andrea and I seem to nitpick every little thing to death." Todd was Robyn's "ops" guy, responsible for the day-to-day running of the business, and Andrea was the senior designer. Robyn's role—in addition to being the founder/owner—was as the main client liaison—the senior "suit."

"I'm frustrated, Les." Another pause. "This isn't what I signed up for. I've never been interested in the business mogul thing—huddled in an office, shooting out orders to people . . . that's not me. You know that. I just want to deliver great design to great clients . . ."

Robyn's voice trailed off, and I knew why. That had been her—and the business's—mantra: "We deliver great design to great clients." Back in the day, she'd said it over and over—and over—again. I knew it meant everything to her. I waited as Robyn formulated her thoughts.

"I had that," she said. "You know I had that." A final pause. "I want it back."

# No More LEGO Tables

Two weeks later, I pulled my rental car into the parking lot of Robyn's Sausalito offices. It hadn't taken much to persuade me to visit with Robyn and her team—they were people I liked working with and it was a place I loved visiting. From the outside, little had changed: the same manicured office park, the same gorgeous view, the same consistently beautiful weather.

Inside, the contrast with the past couldn't have been more different. Instead of the familiar funky, creative workspace, I walked into a chaotic mess. Paper was everywhere—forms, memos, client designs—splayed across disorganized desktops, stacked on top of file cabinets, piled on the floor. The main work area, originally playfully designed with exercise balls as chairs and LEGO tables to encourage creative thinking and collaboration, had been replaced with drab, makeshift cubicles. One sad, partially deflated exercise ball sat against a wall, a silent witness to past glory.

Most striking of all, instead of the exuberant, funky, focused and energized team of people that had greeted me previously, the room was full of tired-looking, harassed multitaskers, all of whom seemed too busy to give an unknown visitor more than a cursory glance. The atmosphere was strained and brittle.

Robyn appeared in the doorway of the conference room at the far side of the main office and beckoned me over with a bland photocopy of her once-glowing smile. I could see Todd and Andrea behind her, seated at the conference table. As we shook hands and Robyn poured coffee, Todd fanned out a set of photocopied documents and slid a copy across the table to each of us. "We're losing money," he said, without introduction. "And we're not sure where. Our financials are too basic to tell us much more than that we're losing money."

Andrea looked up from her morning bagel. "Forget about the money," she said. "We're losing our reputation for high-quality work—and that's much more critical than the money. In this business, without our reputation, we're done." Todd looked daggers at Andrea, looked at me, then looked back to his colleague. "That's typical, Andrea. Forget about the money?" he swiveled toward Robyn. "How can we stay in business if . . ." I put my hand up. This wasn't starting well.

"Hold on, folks. We'll get to all that soon enough. Let's back up a bit." I looked at Robyn, Todd and Andrea. All three of them had tightly clenched jaws. No one was looking at each other. This was a tough time for them.

"Do you remember our last time together, two years ago, when we talked about how your business was at a growth stage called Fun?" They each nodded, Robyn with a wry smile and Todd rolling his eyes. "Do you remember when I explained what comes after Fun—sure as night follows day?" Todd and Andrea looked blank. Robyn made a little bob of her head, intimating that she remembered something—vaguely.

"No . . ." Despite the seriousness of the moment, I couldn't help myself—the single syllable came out as a chuckle. "I didn't expect you would." *People in Fun rarely do*, I thought—and why should they? Fun is such a great stage to be at, and who wants to hear that one day it might— strike that—*will* be over?

"Well, whether or not you remember it, now you're there. Welcome to the next stage of growth. You're in Whitewater."

# What Whitewater Is

Whitewater is the third stage of growth for every organization, after Early Struggle and Fun.

Whitewater occurs as a natural outgrowth from Fun—in other words, an organization doesn't have to do anything specific to get into Whitewater—once it reaches the Fun stage, so long as the organization continues to grow, it will hit Whitewater automatically.

To put it another way: Whitewater comes as an unavoidable corollary of growth. As soon as the small, vibrant organization emerges from Early Struggle into Fun and starts to grow, it immediately begins to become more complex. More people are added, so decision making becomes more difficult. Lines of communication are less clear, making execution difficult also. Additionally, as the business's customer or client list grows, so does the long tail of legacy, or service, issues attached to each customer (something the "new" organization has never had to deal with before) until eventually, the organization is spending more time in dealing with the servicing of past sales than it is in getting or making new ones.

Of course, larger organizations with systems and processes in place find this complexity easier to cope with—the whole purpose of systems and processes is to enable an organization to deal effectively with complexity. The problem is, our young growing organization doesn't have many—if any—processes or systems. It's on the way up, and so far, it hasn't needed any systems or processes; in fact, it sees them as a bad thing: "Hey—we're flexible and we can turn on a dime. We don't have titles, or job descriptions, or rules or systems or processes—they'd just get in our way."

As a result, the Whitewater stage—painful as it is—is often more prolonged than it needs to be, because senior management's natural reaction is to reject the very thing that is needed to get through Whitewater: systems and processes. The logic is simple and compelling: Because systems and processes have until now been anathema ("We're young, vibrant and creatively unstructured"), they are now rejected as a solution to the problems caused by Whitewater. In fact, as we'll see, the right balance of systems and processes—not too few, not too many—is exactly what's required in order to get the business stabilized and take it out of Whitewater.

# The Boiling Frog

Why would a savvy business owner or manager refuse to introduce systems and processes if doing so would stop the boat-rocking of Whitewater that's threatening to capsize the business?

Because Whitewater doesn't happen overnight. The slide into Whitewater is subtle and gradual: Like the frog in cold water that never notices as the water temperature is slowly increased until the poor thing is boiled alive, most business owners and managers don't realize that the water temperature is rising—that they are in fact sliding into Whitewater—let alone that to adjust they need to change their attitude toward systems and process.

Looked at from the perspective of the owner or manager in Fun, the early indicators of Whitewater are merely speed bumps along the road, not a signal that major change is ahead. A missed shipment? Jimmy the warehouse guy was sick that day—a glitch, and it won't happen again. Purchased the wrong Widgets for a big project? Jayne phoned in the order on a crackly line—could happen to anyone. A disappointed customer calling the boss to complain? He was difficult from the outset, and we probably shouldn't have taken his business to begin with.

The answer to these irritants? The same answer as for everything in Fun: Sell more! We're good at that—it's what we do best—and more sales mean more profit, which means more growth. Yes?

As Whitewater gathers pace, the answer increasingly becomes "no." Fast-forward the video to a few months later: The warehouse is now missing at least one delivery date every week. Purchasing returns have continued to rise and are now 11 percent of total purchases. Customer complaints have become frequent enough that they're now being directed to someone other than the boss. At this point, the organization can no longer sell its way out of the problems it faces—in fact, every new sale only makes the situation worse. But yet, because it was the main focus in Fun (and because management hasn't yet realized that Fun is over), the business continues to sell, sell, sell—placing increasingly heavier demands on the rest of the organization's operational (non-sales) functions.

And so as Whitewater builds in intensity, the organization's time and resources are increasingly—and painfully—redirected from the care and feeding of the sales function to firefighting the growing number of errors and emergencies appearing in its operational (non-selling) activities. This has two immediate results: Growth stalls, as the business's focus turns from selling to firefighting internal brush fires; and profitability drops, as the business eats the cost of rectifying its increasingly frequent inefficiencies.

Taken together, these two changes (decline in sales growth and in profitability) push the business into full-blown Whitewater.

# Re-Arranging the Deck Chairs

At this point, where the initial gentle breeze of occasional, explicable "glitches" gives way to the full-blown, side-to-side boat-rocking of Whitewater, senior management has an "Aha!" moment:

In order to stop the tidal wave of errors and mistakes that are crippling its growth and draining its profits, the organization needs to learn how to excel at everything else *but* sales. To stop (or at least drastically reduce) the delivery problems, the purchasing errors and the customer complaints (or whatever combination of operational difficulties the business is facing), the non-sales parts of the business need to receive the same sort of care and attention heretofore reserved almost solely for the sales function.

As a first step, there is usually a redesign of the organization chart, away from the Sun and Moons of Fun (see Figure 3.1) to something that we might say looks more like a "Heart and Kidney."

In fact, this is not a "redesign" but the first time an organization chart is drawn up at all. Until now, through Early Struggle and Fun, the organization chart, if it exists at all, is simply a notional idea, included perhaps in a business plan as a matter of form. Whitewater is usually when the idea of the organization chart as a genuine tool for management first arises.

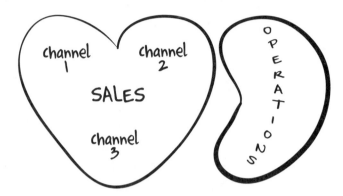

Figure 4.1 The Heart and the Kidney

As we've seen, up until now all the non-sales functions have existed as independent "satellites." Until now, their only purpose has been to service the wants and needs of the sales function. The organization's main focus has been on the care and feeding of the sales function, and everything else has been subordinated to that.

So the first step in retooling the non-sales functions is to consolidate most or all of these functions into a division or department of their own, and to appoint an "operations manager" to oversee this new entity—as in Figure 4.1 above. This has the seeming logic of simplifying the complexity and lack of transparency that has caused the operational problems in the first place. As an ancillary benefit the CEO (or, more likely at this stage, the owner/manager), who has been increasingly run ragged while hopping from fire to fire, now has a single point of control over what were previously a large number of small independent fiefdoms.

And so someone internally—a particularly good "satellite" function manager, perhaps the long-suffering accountant or warehouse manager—or, less often, an external hire is appointed to manage the all-new "Ops Function" (or whatever it may be called). Let's call this manager Jack. Jack is briefed on his new portfolio of responsibilities—all or most of the non-sales functions—and given an explicit directive to introduce whatever systems and processes are necessary to stop the brush fires. All seems well, the problem has been identified, the logical steps have been taken to fix the problem and now—back to Fun: more sales and more growth! Yes?

# Not So Fast

Well, maybe not. Let's run the video forward again—say, nine to twelve months into the future (cue time-travel music) . . .

As the mists of time swirl, what do we see? There's Jack, the ops manager, sitting in his office, staring stony-faced at his computer screen. He appears to be muttering. We're not close enough to hear what Jack is saying, but it's clear he's not a happy camper. He appears to be reading an email that's making him very cross. Let's zoom in a little . . .

Ah yes, it is indeed an email, and it's from Jill, the GM of Sales (she was appointed to this position at about the same time as Jack was made GM of Ops). Jill has sent the email to Jack and copied it to Fred, who is the owner and president of the company. Jill is complaining bitterly about the new system Jack has implemented, which requires a copy of every sales order to be sent to the purchasing department within 24 hours of the sale being made. It's not easy to read the screen from here, but if we move closer, we may be able to make out a few snatches from the email: ". . . paid to sell, not complete your endless paperwork . . ."; ". . . just one more example of micromanaging . . ."; ". . . not your department . . ."; ". . . how can we be expected to . . ."; ". . . asking us to do your job for you."

Hmm. Now Jack is replying . . . Yes, he's hit REPLY TO ALL, plus he's added a couple of additional names in the CC box for good measure. Oh, and one in the BCC box too. Nice touch. Let's follow along as he types: ". . . cavalier mavericks who can't spell T-E-A-M"; ". . . no respect for others"; ". . . shoddy, incomplete and unreadable paperwork"; ". . . how can we be expected to . . ."; ". . . do I need to remind you of the last time your people . . ."; ". . . countless occasions when my team has bailed out this organization." Tough stuff. Jack hesitates. Will he hit SEND, or will he relent? The screen fades . . .

# Sales Versus Operations

Jack, Jill and Fred have been caught by a common trap that ensnares most organizations when they first try to deal with Whitewater—the "sales versus operations" battle of attrition.

Watching Jack and Jill fight it out, it's probable that Fred believes this tetchy relationship is simply a personality issue between Jack and Jill, and the answer (equally simply) is that they need their heads banged together. But the fact is, whatever the quality of their personal relationship, Jack and Jill were doomed to fall into trench warfare, thanks to the organization structure that had been adopted a year earlier. Let's take a closer look at the Heart and Kidney:

Figure 4.2 No Man's Land

See that "no man's land"—the gap in the middle, running all the way between "sales" and "ops"? Now, imagine there is a problem—with a customer, say, who is still waiting for the product the nice salesman promised would be delivered three weeks ago. Guess where that (relatively simple, and not uncommon) problem sits? With the "heart"—sales, for over-promising on the delivery date? Or with the

> There isn't room here to go into all the reasons why neither sales nor ops will take responsibility for issues that land in no man's land—a detailed discussion must wait for a later book—but the key reasons are the relative newness of the respective roles, the lack of clear escalation processes and the impact of the Big Dogs (which we do discuss later in this chapter).

"kidney"—operations, for failing to deliver on time? Or maybe both sales and ops are stepping up and jointly taking responsibility?

The answer of course, is "none of the above." In fact the problem—along with 90 percent of all the *other* problems the business is fighting—is sitting right there in no man's land, orphaned, unloved, uncared for and certainly not about to be fixed any time soon. How can a problem be fixed if no one is first taking responsibility for it?

# The Big Dogs Raise Their Heads

At this point in the organization's development there is more angst, tension and infighting than at any time previously. Functional groups hunker down in their silos, act in an increasingly insular manner and hoard information. As we've seen, issues increasingly fall between the cracks—or more precisely, fall into the no man's land created by the new organization chart. Distrust and paranoia grow between the sales and ops functions.

In this atmosphere—where at best, the sales and ops functions are dysfunctional, and at worst, there is almost civil war between them—there is one striking difference between the two sides: access to power. The sales function, remember, has its Big Dogs—the superstars, who through their loyalty and derring-do helped build the business in the early days, and who are an integral part of the myths and legends of the organization. They have their sweat equity, and through that, access to the center of power—the ear of the founder, owner or senior management.

The ops function, on the other hand, is brand-new and has no sweat equity, and consequently has an entirely different type of access. While they may meet formally or informally with management, the senior ops staff typically don't have the bonds built by a strong prior relationship, and are therefore in a weaker position to influence decisions.

The sales function, in other words, can use its Big Dogs to mount a strong lobbying campaign in the sales versus ops battle. This gives sales staff an often insurmountable edge, as they whisper to management, "Look at the mess all these systems and processes have gotten us into." "I can't get to see customers anymore, with all the paperwork and the meetings

I'm now expected to attend." "Remember how simple it used to be—and how profitable we were then?" "These ops folks just don't get it—none of them has ever made a sale in their life."

Guess what the Big Dogs would like to see happen? A return to Fun, of course (salespeople *love* Fun)—and most specifically, a return to the Sun and Moons, sales-centric organization chart. Back to the time when sales snapped its finger and everyone else jumped.

## The Founder's Dilemma

This is an important decision point for management—most particularly, for the founder. At this stage, all the angst caused by the sales versus ops clash, coupled with an accompanying steep decline in self-accountability and initiative in the workforce—and with the added impact of the constant drip of the Big Dog lobbying campaign—can combine to frustrate management to such an extent that it dismantles the entire Heart and Kidney system, trying in effect to return directly to Fun by reverting to the sales-centric Sun and Moons structure.

The logic is tempting, even compelling: Things were good previously things are bad now, so let's go back to what we were doing before. It's understandable that the business owner or senior management should at least consider this option—of returning to Fun—and many do. The alternative, after all, is exceptionally painful: The prospect of staying the course, holding the ring for the sales and ops folks to battle it out, continuing to deal with all this conflict is not only unpleasant, it also seems interminable—there's no light at the end of the tunnel.

Added to that, for many managers, this seemingly insuperable problem—Whitewater—causes them to doubt their own management skills, leading them to wonder if they've "got what it takes" to manage a business of this size.

And so, for many owners and managers, the simplest thing to do at this point is to reverse course, unwind the organizational changes, try to put the genie back in the bottle and return to the days of sales-centric Fun. The ops function is dismantled as a single entity, the individual functions go back to operating independently and sales is restored to primacy. All is well. For a while. And then the brush fires start again: dropped deliveries, out-of-stock inventory, unhappy customers . . .

Because here's the catch: As soon as the organization simplifies itself and returns to Fun, the sales function once more flourishes, and the business immediately starts to grow again. As a result of the growth, complexity begins to creep back in, and history repeats itself—Whitewater begins once more. Another attempt is made on the Heart and Kidney approach—this time, management is older and wiser, so it chooses "better" people and manages the process more intimately, but lo and behold, with the same result: sales versus ops, as each retreat into their dysfunctional silos.

Sometimes an organization can go through this cycle—bobbing in and out of Whitewater and Fun—many times, each time trying some different way to introduce systems and processes that will manage the complexities of growth, and each time meeting with the same resistance, the same intransigence, the same Whitewater.

As a result, some owners decide to stop trying to beat Whitewater altogether, and instead permanently cap the growth of their business to let them stay firmly in Fun, resisting the temptation to go beyond the revenue or staffing levels that cause Whitewater—a dynamic often called the Founder's Dilemma. Many excellent businesses (and most successful mom-and-pop operations) have made this decision, and if managed correctly, they can live on to enjoy Fun indefinitely.

## Getting Out of Whitewater

But what of the founder or management team that doesn't want to cap growth? Are they destined to suffer the dysfunctions of Whitewater indefinitely? Clearly not—many organizations make it out of Whitewater and into Predictable Success—so, what is the secret of getting out of Whitewater?

The answer, as with so much that we've seen already, lies in creating the right organization structure—building an underlying foundation for success by providing the right framework for people to work within.

Specifically, the organization structure required to move a business out of Whitewater and into Predictable Success is one in which the no man's land between sales and operations is extinguished. It usually looks something like this, and for obvious reasons, I call it the "Catcher's Mitt":

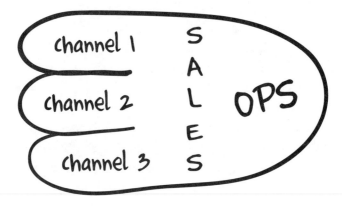

Figure 4.3 The Catcher's Mitt

Here, rather than having sales and operations as disconnected islands with a gaping void between them, the two functions, though clearly identifiably separate, are linked together. This brings with it two major benefits for the organization:

- There are no cracks for issues and problems to "fall between"— within this organization structure, everything gets "caught" somewhere.

- There is a clear "line of sight" between all parts of the organization, making it much harder for insular silos to form.

Getting an organization out of Whitewater by shifting its structure from the Heart and Kidney model to the Catcher's Mitt is a specific process with clearly identifiable steps, and as such is worthy of a chapter in its own right (Chapter 9: Almost There—Breaking Through Whitewater into Predictable Success), and if you wish to explore this transition in more detail I recommend you skip to Chapter 9 once you are finished with this chapter.

However, before we leave the Catcher's Mitt, let's consider this question: Whenever management realizes the business has hit Whitewater, shouldn't the organization go straight to the Catcher's Mitt structure, and bypass the Heart and Kidney stage altogether?

Well, the theoretical answer is "yes"—it obviously would be preferable if the business could avoid the strain of the sales versus ops battle altogether; but the reality (as you might guess) is somewhat more complicated. Here are the main reasons why the Heart and Kidney stage often cannot be avoided:

1. The logic of the Heart and Kidney—that it simplifies and adds transparency to the system—is compelling.

2. Managers of an organization in Whitewater are usually relatively inexperienced, learning the effects of organizational change as they go along. Facing Whitewater for the first time, they have no experience (and can therefore have no knowledge of) the likely problems the Heart and Kidney model will cause.

3. Making the transition to Heart and Kidney is in itself a very large change—moving right away to the Catcher's Mitt is almost inconceivable for most management teams coming out of Fun.

4. As we shall see in Chapter 9, the management team almost always lacks some of the core skills necessary to make the Catcher's Mitt work (notably, working cross-functionally and building peer relationships). Ironically, it is during the time spent grappling with the problems caused by the Heart and Kidney that the management team will build the muscle needed to make the Catcher's Mitt work later.

# Working for an Organization in Whitewater

For an employee (let alone management), working for an organization in Whitewater is often the most difficult phase of all—much worse even than Death Rattle. Days are stressful, the organization is dysfunctional, it feels as though the business has lost its identity and there is no sense of direction. Management seems to be changing the rules of the game frequently—every month brings a new mantra, a new fad, a new "must do" focus. There is little sense of job satisfaction—nothing feels as if it is ever good enough, and it's very hard to see how or where your own individual activity is contributing to the wider success of the organization as a whole.

During Whitewater the organization often experiences its first serious levels of employee turnover. As a "them and us" attitude develops between sales and operations, some of the more loyal non-sales employees leave or are pushed out. In its desire to ensure a greater adherence to systems and processes, management replaces those who leave with people from larger organizations who are more accustomed to working with—and more comfortable with—systems and processes than were the more loyal "old-timers."

As a result of this, a second front opens up—now, in addition to the sales versus ops feud, a gulf begins to emerge between the old-timers and the new hires, with the veterans complaining that "nothing is the same around here anymore" and talking increasingly about how it was "back in the day." The new hires, for their part, view the veterans as dinosaurs with antediluvian work practices, and wonder aloud as to how the organization was ever successful before they arrived to the rescue.

All of this leads to a serious reduction in morale, which in turn accelerates the loss of the loyal, family-like, go-getter, flexible culture that had developed in Fun. Often managers will become increasingly less visible, retreating to their offices rather than face yet more dysfunction. Several false dawns can appear, as management increasingly swings for the fences in an attempt to stop what feels like an inexorable collapse of the business.

## SUMMARY

- Whitewater is the third stage in every organization's development, after Early Struggle and Fun.
- Whitewater arrives as a natural outgrowth from the success of Fun.
- The main cause of Whitewater is complexity arising from growth.
- It is evidenced by increasing errors and emergencies in the organization.
- Management rarely recognizes the arrival of Whitewater—it thinks the errors and emergencies are merely "bumps in the road."
- When it does address Whitewater, management's first reaction is often to go to a "Heart and Kidney" organization structure.
- This only makes the situation worse, with a "no man's land" fueling an increasingly vitriolic "sales versus operations" conflict.
- Some founders and owners choose to take their organizations permanently back to Fun.
- Other organizations bob in and out of Fun and Whitewater, repeating each of the steps above.
- The only way to move forward out of Whitewater is by shifting to the "Catcher's Mitt" organization structure.
- During Whitewater, the organization's focus shifts from sales to profitability.
- Working for an organization in Whitewater is highly stressful and leads to high employee turnover.

# [ CHAPTER FIVE ]

## PREDICTABLE SUCCESS: ACHIEVING PERFECT BALANCE—SUCCEED, LEARN, REPEAT

"When you put your foot on the gas in this company, the car goes forward."
—Jeff Immelt, CEO, GE

IT WAS INCREDIBLE TO WATCH.

I was standing inside a hangar the size of two football fields, still waiting for my toes to thaw from the cold outside. To my left on a long, flat trestle table were stacked six or seven enormous slabs of inanimate lumber, each bigger than a man. Beside me stood Ian, my host for the day and the owner of the business. Six foot three and with an easy, lazy grin, he was clearly enjoying this.

Ian reached over to a plastic-encased keyboard on the side of the trestle table, punched in a single keystroke and stood back with the proud expression of a parent watching his child perform at the school play. With a quiet hiss, the first of the slabs of lumber slid forward on the work surface and into an area behind a transparent, protective plastic screen.

Behind the screen four robotic arms appeared and, in an industrial version of *Dancing With the Stars*, briskly lifted, turned, cut, shaped and gently replaced the slab of wood, now clearly recognizable as an ornate—if as yet unfinished—entry door.

As the industrial robots worked relentlessly through the pile of lumber—just under seven minutes per door, each door a perfect replica of the last—Ian arched an eyebrow, gave me a "you ain't seen nuthin' yet" look and motioned me to follow him round to the back of the unit. "Look at this," he said, pointing to the cast-off strips of wood the robot was stacking to one side.

I wasn't sure what I was meant to notice. It seemed the least impressive part of the operation. "Scrap wood—okayyyy . . . Umm . . . nice stacking?" I couldn't think of much else to say.

"Nope. That's the point—this isn't scrap," Ian said as he pointed further left, to a bin containing a tiny pile of dust, splinters, and one or two small offcuts. "That's the scrap. This first pile"—pointing back to the larger offcuts—"is finished parts we will use in the door frame construction. The robot is programmed with the specification for every piece needed for the door and the door frame, so it's able to scan each individual piece of raw lumber and compute a cutting pattern that maximizes the amount of usable wood. Sometimes we can get the door itself plus eight or nine additional parts, just from one piece of lumber. My waste wood used to be nearly 25 percent—now it's down to single figures."

Ian shot me his lazy grin again. He and I both knew that impressive as it was, this was about more—much more—than just saving scrap wood. It was emblematic of how he had transformed his entire business. The precision, elegance, dependability and breathtaking efficiency of this giant door-producing robot was also a stunning metaphor for the rebirth of Ian's business that had happened when he and his team, over four long, painful years, had pulled his organization out of Whitewater into Predictable Success. Just a short time previously, this was an organization for which the very notion of efficient profitability and growth was unthinkable.

# A Trip to the ICU

As we walked to another part of the factory so I could be shown the new process for painting and finishing the doors, I glanced through one of the few windows at the snow-covered car park outside. The factory was located in Michigan, and the lake effect meant the snow was drifting deep. As had happened so often over the last four years, there was a strong possibility that my travel plans would be upended.

Not that I minded—over the years Ian had become a friend as well as a client, and we enjoyed each other's company. If the airport closed, a pleasant meal in a local Italian restaurant was our usual response.

Our relationship hadn't started so cordially. When a mutual friend first recommended that I meet with Ian, his business was deep in Whitewater, and he was under a lot of pressure. When I was shown into his office, he was buried—almost literally—in paperwork and hassled by his employees, and he displayed none of the languid grace and good humor I later came to know as the "real" Ian.

As I stood waiting, Ian had barely looked up from his computer. "I don't believe in miracle cures," he snapped. Nice opener. "Neither do I . . . ," I said. Ian turned and nodded me toward a chair. ". . . but I do believe in intensive care therapy," I continued, "and I think your business needs just that." Ian paused, looked at me intently—and smiled, albeit weakly. "Okay . . . Doc"—there was more than a little sarcasm in the way he drew out the word—"tell me more. What would this intensive care therapy of yours look like?"

Over Ian's shoulder, I could see the screen of his computer, displaying his email. The whole of the upper screen was filled with bold, unread subject lines. "Well, I need to know a bit more about your business, Ian. Can I ask you some specific questions?" I pulled out my yellow pad.

During that morning as we spoke, the list of unread emails grew one by one, each time accompanied by a barely audible "ping." As I listened to Ian share the history of his door and window manufacturing business, the low, slow, repetitive "ping . . . ping . . . ping" sounded like a heart monitor, underlining the urgency of helping Ian find a solution to Whitewater.

Ian shared with me his by now familiar story: After a tough early few years gaining traction in an already crowded industry, he'd secured a major customer in the hospitality industry. Getting that customer had kick-started his business's fast growth, which in turn led to expansion into a new factory, new product line extension and of course, sales, sales, sales.

Then, inevitably, Whitewater. Ian had woken up one day to find the bank banging on his door: Profits had declined and cash flow was drying up; customers were going elsewhere because quality and delivery times had declined, and worst of all, the highly motivated, loyal team that had worked through thick and thin to get the business through Early Struggle and Fun was fragmenting and key employees were leaving.

"What gets to me most," said Ian, clearly struggling with his emotions, "is that I can't even take pride in what we're doing anymore." He got up from his seat. "Come here," he said, flinging open a side door that led from his office directly onto the factory floor. "Look at that." I followed to where his finger was pointing—a series of long, low tables, where about twenty or twenty-five workers were clustered around large slabs of lumber. Or so I calculated by looking at their heads and shoulders, because their lower bodies were completely obscured by offcuts of wood. "You see all that wood stacked on the floor? That's wasted wood—that's my profit—gone."

Ian shut the door and returned to his desk, explaining how the loss of key people, the sheer volume of work they had taken on and the generally chaotic state of the business meant that they were producing doors almost at a loss—the volume of waste wood was only the most obvious part of a loss-making production process that leaked like a sieve.

When Ian had finished answering my questions, always politely but with obvious skepticism, it was my turn to talk. I explained each of the stages in development that every organization goes through, then doubled back to take him through Early Struggle, Fun and Whitewater in more detail. As I did so, Ian—slowly at first, and then more frequently—nodded in recognition of many of his own experiences. Eventually, he reached over for a pad of paper and began to take notes.

Finally, I outlined what it meant for an organization to push through Whitewater into Predictable Success.

Then I gave him the good news: "Ian, this may seem counterintuitive, just when you think your business is coming apart. But the fact is, if you handle Whitewater correctly, your business will never have been in better shape. You're just one step away from Predictable Success."

He looked down at the notes he had been taking. "And if I get it wrong, I could slide in and out of Whitewater indefinitely, right?" I nodded. Ian was a quick learner. He paused. A quiet "ping" announced the arrival of yet another email. "Okay, Les. Let's say I want to get it right. That I want to get to Predictable Success. What do I do?"

Now, for the first time that morning, Ian was fully engaged. He saw the future, and he wanted it. "It'll take me a little time to explain," I said, "and it's almost lunchtime."

Ian looked at his watch. "You like Italian?"

# What Predictable Success Is

Predictable Success is the fourth stage in the organization's development, coming after Early Struggle, Fun and Whitewater. The transition from Whitewater to Predictable Success is achieved by introducing and maintaining the right amount of systems and processes necessary to tame complexity, while at the same time holding in balance the entrepreneurial zeal, creativity and risk taking that have grown the business to this point.

The definition of an organization in Predictable Success is that it has the ability to readily set and consistently achieve its goals. In fact, at no other stage in its development will the organization be more in control of its own destiny—when an organization reaches Predictable Success, it is at the point of maximum self-determination.

This is not to say that it has reached a state of error-free perfection. Just like any other complex entity, the Predictable Success organization is far from perfect—it will make mistakes, hit roadblocks and be just as exposed to the impact of external events beyond its control as any other organization. The difference is in how the Predictable Success organization *responds* to those difficulties.

When an organization in Predictable Success does hit problems, either external or internal, it responds in a manner that is unique to this stage in development: It maturely assesses the impact of the problem, decides on the optimal response, executes that response with minimal drama, and swiftly returns its focus to its underlying priorities and goals.

## Being Like Water

This focused, no-drama response to problems and obstacles is a key identifier of an organization in Predictable Success: Management refuses to be distracted unnecessarily, crisis mode is rarely invoked and the organization restabilizes after problem solving, with minimal drama.

Productivity guru David Allen (channeling Bruce Lee—Allen is also a martial arts practitioner) calls it "being like water." His point is this: When a stone is dropped into the sea or a pond, the resulting ripples are no more or no less than the required reaction to the arriving object. The body of water has no interest in the motives of the stone thrower and takes no offense at the arrival of the stone—it simply reacts as physics dictates: absorbing the stone, producing ripples, then returning to its previous state.

The Predictable Success organization responds similarly to issues and problems—with no more and no less of a response than is necessary, dissipating the impact with only the required amount of disruption before returning quickly to balance.

Put another way, Predictable Success is that stage in development where the organization is most at ease with itself, is most assured of its identity and purpose, and executes its business with the self-confidence and fluidity of an athlete at the top of his or her game. When in Predictable Success, organizations exhibit what the prolific psychology professor Mihaly Csikszentmihalyi calls "flow"—a confluence of enjoyment, creativity, precision and total involvement that produces outstanding results.

Theoretically, once it has arrived at Predictable Success, there is no reason why an organization should not stay there, continuing to "be like water," exhibiting flow and producing outstanding results indefinitely. Yet while many organizations do stay in Predictable Success for extended periods of time, experience demonstrates that most eventually either become overdependent on systems and processes (and hence slide forward into Treadmill), or lose the discipline of enforcing those same systems and processes, causing the organization to slide back into Whitewater.

# Staying in Predictable Success: An Exquisite Tension

The reason for this is that staying in Predictable Success is hard work. Despite its seeming ease, the flow that Predictable Success organizations demonstrate outwardly is not achieved lightly—in fact, being in Predictable Success is a great example of something that looks easy on the surface, but is considerably more complicated behind the scenes. While to an outside observer the management of an organization in Predictable Success may appear as simple as putting one foot in front of another, in truth, just as with the act of walking, there is a lot going on beneath the surface.

At the core of Predictable Success is an ever-present, ever-shifting tension that holds two competing but equally necessary forces in a fine balance: On the one hand are the creativity, drive, initiative and entrepreneurial spirit that give the organization its vision, and on the other are the precise and mundane systems and processes that bring scalability, consistency and profitability.

These two forces must coexist in the right proportions to maintain an organization in the state of Predictable Success. If on the one hand creativity and entrepreneurial zeal dominate and drive out the systems and processes, the organization will slide back down to Whitewater. Alternatively, if the bean counters take over, and systems and processes begin to squeeze out initiative and risk taking, then (as we shall see in the next chapter) the organization will slide forward into Treadmill.

For management, holding this tension in balance is rather like steering a sailboat: Due to tides and winds, it doesn't work to simply point the boat toward a desired location and then sit back and enjoy the view. The destination can be reached only by constantly making adjustments, tacking the boat back and forth. So it is with the Predictable Success organization—it stays in Predictable Success only so long as the right adjustments are being made in the constantly shifting balance between entrepreneurial fervor and administrative precision.

This means that in Predictable Success there can be no acceptance of the status quo. Any sense that the organization has "arrived" and can relax or rest on its laurels is fatal to the organization's continuance in Predictable Success. Changes in the market environment, in personnel, in the supply chain, in legislation, in technology and in a hundred other areas occur daily—sometimes hourly—and the Predictable Success organization must react to those changes by constantly adjusting and readjusting the intricate and delicate balance between creativity and systems, between vision and process. We'll examine in detail how the organization does so in Chapter 11: Staying at the Peak—Maintaining Predictable Success Once You Get There.

## The Key Benefits of Predictable Success

Although there are many benefits to an organization that reaches Predictable Success, four are key:

1. Relative ease of decision making
2. Alignment of decision making and execution
3. Effective cross-functional interaction across the organization
4. A coequal focus on growth and profitability

Taken together, these four benefits combine over time to develop a fifth, transcendent competitive advantage:

5. An intuitive, institutionalized understanding of how the organization succeeds.

Let's take a deeper look at each of these in turn:

## 1. RELATIVE EASE OF DECISION MAKING.

While in Whitewater, the organization's decision making is confused and inefficient; in Treadmill it is brittle and ineffective. But in Predictable Success, the organization can make decisions that are both timely and (relatively) easily reached.

> All four of these key characteristics are examined in detail in Chapter 9: Almost There—Breaking Through Whitewater into Predictable Success, and Chapter 11: Staying at the Peak—Maintaining Predictable Success Once You Get There.

This ability to absorb, analyze and act on data to produce high-quality decisions is achieved through a combination of clarified management roles and responsibilities, the enhanced ability of managers (indeed, all employees) to work cross-functionally, and the decentralization of decision-making processes. As each of these are implemented, together they combine to turn the organization chart (which in Whitewater is unclear and ambiguous if it exists at all, and in Treadmill is a map of fiefdoms) into what is meant to be: a machine for decision making.

## 2. ALIGNMENT OF DECISION MAKING AND EXECUTION.

There are two stages to achieving results in business: first, making the right decisions to begin with (see above), and second, implementing those decisions effectively.

In Whitewater, the gap is wide between the original decisions made (or plans set in place) and the actual results. In Whitewater, because of management's Fun-grown desire to "fix the problem" with one big home run or with a single bold initiative, the organization's budgets or targets tend to consist of BHAGs—big, hairy, audacious goals—with little detail attached, and the actual results achieved often bear little or no relationship to those goals.

In Treadmill, conversely, the gap between plans and actual results is suspiciously small. A slick, rolling budgeting process, an ingrained CYA ("cover your ass") mentality, and the demand for daily, weekly and monthly reports mean that the budgets (the original decisions) and the actual results are constantly massaged to always appear to be close, disguising any real trends that genuine data would reveal.

In Predictable Success, decision making (including forecasting, budgeting and planning) and execution are linked together seamlessly to propel the business forward. Because the organization chart is designed in such a way as to ensure that decision makers and implementers are as close as possible—and as a consequence, true delegation leads to employee empowerment—the timely and informed goal-setting process described above is accompanied by effective and efficient execution. Finally, because the organization's feedback loop is timely and objectively accurate, plans are regularly and consistently reviewed in the light of actual results, and necessary corrections (upward and downward) are made as needed.

## 3. EFFECTIVE CROSS-FUNCTIONAL INTERACTION ACROSS THE ORGANIZATION.

Watching the interaction of the different functional groups of an organization in Predictable Success is rather like watching a highly trained relay team hand the baton from one runner to the next: They can do it seamlessly, over and over again, at high speed, and without looking back.

Compared to the organization in Whitewater, where the baton is constantly being dropped in the no man's land between sales and ops (see Figure 4.2), and in Treadmill, where protective, insular silos increasingly erect barriers to effective interaction, the organization in Predictable Success can pass the baton right across the business: from R&D to marketing, from marketing to sales, from sales to fulfillment, and from fulfillment to service, with minimal fumbling. This of course means not only high customer satisfaction and high employee engagement, but also higher-than-average profits, as losses from inefficiencies are minimized.

## 4. A COEQUAL FOCUS ON GROWTH AND PROFITABILITY.

In Fun, the organization is focused primarily on top-line revenue growth, and in Whitewater, it is concerned primarily with restoring profitability. In Treadmill, when the organization begins to lose its entrepreneurial mojo, as we shall see in the next chapter, management turns its primary focus to ROI (the unspoken argument being "We no longer know how to grow this business, so we better squeeze the most we can from what we have").

When it is in Predictable Success, the organization learns how to walk and chew gum at the same time: Because of the systems and processes it has in place, it can deliver revenue growth without allowing complexity (and the resultant inefficiencies) to depress bottom-line profitability. Because the organization is still entrepreneurial and visionary, it can deliver growth even while reaping a good return on its assets, and (except as part of a defined and temporary strategy) neither growth nor return is pursued at the expense of the other.

## 5. AN UNDERSTANDING OF HOW TO SUCCEED.

After the first, early stages of Predictable Success, as the four characteristics we've examined above begin to take effect, something new begins to emerge in the organization: an intuitive yet institutionalized understanding of how the organization succeeds. It's as if during Predictable Success, as good decisions are made and implemented, as the organization works together cross-functionally, and as growth and profitability accrue as a result, the business develops an organizational "brain"—it learns the patterns of what it needs to do to succeed, and over time, that learning, those patterns, become "baked in," until eventually an understanding of "how and why we are successful" becomes part of the organization's DNA.

Contrast this with the last time the organization was highly successful—in Fun. During Fun, the organization grows quickly, but it never quite knows how or why it is achieving that growth. To misuse a sports metaphor, the organization in Fun is rather like a journeyman golfer finding himself unexpectedly on top of the leaderboard going into the final day of a big tournament. How he got there is a surprise, even to him, and what will happen next is anyone's guess—he may pull out a spectacular victory, or he may implode—who knows? More important, the result that day is no indicator of what might happen the next week or the week after that—there isn't yet a pattern of Predictable Success.

Conversely, the organization in Predictable Success is like a golfer (or any athlete) who has won dozens of tournaments, and who has been ahead on the final day many, many times—this athlete knows precisely what he or she had to do to get there, what's ahead, and what to do next to close out the game and win.

Developing this "muscle memory" of success—building an intuitive, *institutionalized* understanding of how to succeed that isn't dependent on any one individual for execution—is the single biggest benefit of Predictable Success for any organization, as it delivers an imposing competitive advantage.

# Bringing Your People with You

For almost every organization (there are exceptions, but they are few), getting to Predictable Success requires a transformation of many elements of the organization's culture. We've already seen examples of this:

- The shift from out-and-out entrepreneurial zeal to zeal plus process-driven consistency

- The dethroning of the Big Dogs

- The move away from a dependence on individuals for risk taking and creativity, and toward an "institutionalization" of these traits

- The development of the organization's structure from the centralized, static, Sun and Moons model to the decentralized, fluid Catcher's Mitt model

Taken individually, the items in the list above may seem mundane and prosaic, but taken together (along with the many other changes we'll explore in Chapters 9 and 11), they have a profound effect on what it feels like to work in the organization. Individuals who once had a fixed position in the organizational "pecking order" based on loyalty and longevity now find they are competing in a meritocracy; managers and supervisors who became so by receiving "battlefield promotions" during Fun and White-water find that the expectations of their management skills have increased exponentially; team leaders and department heads who formerly were required only to "manage down" to their team now find they must engage horizontally with their peers and colleagues.

None of this comes easy. At the outset of Predictable Success, most people in the organization will have been recruited during Fun and Whitewater, and this—the third—transformation of the organization's culture can be a step too far for some people. As we've seen, when the organization first moves into Predictable Success there is likely to already be tension between the "Fun veterans" and the "Whitewater administrators" over the need for reliance on systems and processes, with the veterans feeling constricted and subdued and the newbie administrators feeling marginalized and unloved. The realization that the organization has moved into yet another phase can be one bridge too many for some employees.

To retain the support of as many of the organization's people as possible, five key steps are required of senior management in managing the transition to Predictable Success:

## 1. EXPLAIN PREDICTABLE SUCCESS.

Most employees will have no overarching concept of what has been happening to the organization they work for. They have not been thinking in terms of organizational life cycles, Fun, Whitewater or anything else of that nature—for them, this is no more or no less than a highly confusing, worrying period when it seems as though the very fabric of the organization has been torn apart by dysfunctional management. Some (in my experience, most) managers will feel the same way.

One of the simplest but most powerful steps senior management can take in the early stages of Predictable Success (or even in Whitewater if they are visionary enough to see the benefit) is to have a town hall: an all-staff meeting in which the principles of Predictable Success are outlined to everyone. Doing so gives a name to the experiences the organization has been through; enables everyone to realize that, far from being "weird," "odd" or highly dysfunctional, the organization has in fact been going through stages that *every* organization goes through; and gives everyone in the organization a common vocabulary to help solve problems and make decisions. (Words are powerful. Being able to share that a certain way of treating a customer, say, was appropriate in Fun, but is not in Predictable Success, can substitute for many hours of uncertain and ambiguous explanation.)

## 2. MAKE IT CLEAR THAT GOING BACK TO WHITEWATER AND FUN IS NOT AN OPTION.

Some employees—particularly those who have worked for the organization for some time—will have a deep attachment to "how it used to be." For those in particular who worked for the organization when it was in Fun, it can seem that *those* were the organization's glory days, and that ever since then, the organization has been going backward. Their motto is "Back to the future"—their only answer is in peeling away this dangerous intrusion of systems and process and returning to Fun.

It is important that such employees—be they managers or individual contributors—not only come to understand the overall life cycle through which the organization is developing (see the point above), but also hear, loud and clear, that it is not an option for the organization to return to Whitewater, let alone Fun. It is vitally important that this message comes from a senior management team that is seen to be united and unanimous. As we shall see in Chapter 11, a single recalcitrant senior manager, demonstrating by word or body language that he or she is less than committed to staying in Predictable Success, can be the catalyst for a swift and precipitous descent back into Whitewater.

## 3. OVERTLY SUPPORT, AFFIRM AND MODEL THE IMPORTANCE OF ADHERENCE TO PROCESS.

It cannot be overemphasized that in leading people from Whitewater to Predictable Success, words are not enough. Every employee is watching avidly to see if senior management really "means it"—and employees will gauge the answer to that question not by management's words, but by its deeds. Talk of adherence to systems and processes is meaningless if at the same time management is failing to adhere to those same systems and processes, or worse still, agreeing to allow certain employees—often the

Big Dogs—to buck the system by ignoring, avoiding or diluting their new administrative responsibilities.

Supporting and modeling adherence to process requires the use of both reward and consequence. Publicly encouraging and praising those who have mastered (better still, improved) new processes is very important—but it is equally important that noncompliance has known consequences, and that those consequences are seen to be applied consistently and with rigor.

## 4. ACCEPT THAT MANY OF YOUR PEOPLE WILL STILL LEAVE.

Despite all of management's best intentions, and even with the application of the steps outlined above, a number of employees—possibly even a large number—will find the transition to Predictable Success simply too much to take and will leave the organization. A combination of those who don't like the new culture, those who feel marginalized or forgotten, and those who don't have the skills required to work in the Predictable Success environment can mean that as many as one-third of the total workforce might turn over during the first few years in Predictable Success.

It's important for management to recognize that, so long as it has engaged in the steps detailed above, this is "healthy" turnover: The organization is moving on, and it's only to be expected that some people will not want to come along for this next stage of the journey. Expensive as it may be in the short term to absorb the impact of such turnover, in the medium- and long-term the organization is better served by having a workforce that is motivated and inspired to uphold the culture of Predictable Success.

## 5. ENSURE THAT THE HIRING PROCESS REFLECTS THE ORGANIZATION'S CULTURE SHIFT.

Every healthy organization has inflows and outflows of personnel—people move on and are replaced by new blood, otherwise the organization stagnates. As we've just seen, moving into Predictable Success is one of those times when this process is accelerated—the cultural transition that the organization goes through will produce a higher-than-usual turnover of departing employees. As a result, hiring will accelerate also, as management seeks to fill the now empty positions.

If management is to avoid perpetuating and extending the turnover in the organization, it is important that the hiring process be retooled to reflect the changes that the organization has gone through. Specifically, the typical hiring style in Fun (visceral, "I like the cut of your jib," attitude-based hiring, usually made directly by the owner/manager) must be replaced with a more—yes—systematic hiring *process* that uses clear job descriptions, behaviorally based questions and panel interviews to identify candidates who will bring not only a great attitude to the organization, but also the ability to easily comply with minimal administrative processes with ease.

## SUMMARY

- Predictable Success is the fourth stage in any organization's development, after Early Struggle, Fun and Whitewater.

- Predictable Success is achieved by introducing the systems and processes needed for the organization to conquer complexity and get out of Whitewater.

- When in Predictable Success, the organization is at its prime and can readily set and consistently achieve its goals.

- Theoretically, if the right balance of systems and processes is maintained, there is no reason why an organization cannot remain in Predictable Success indefinitely.

- Allowing the newly introduced systems and processes to lapse (or to be bypassed) can lead to the organization sliding back into Whitewater.

- Introducing too many systems and processes, or depending on systems and processes to substitute for initiative and creativity, will push the organization forward into Treadmill.

- Management's key role is to maintain the right balance between vision and process so the organization remains in Predictable Success.

- The ability to make and implement decisions with relative ease in turn builds a competitive advantage, as the organization slowly institutionalizes its ability to succeed.

- Management must explain, support and model the actions necessary for the organization to remain in Predictable Success, particularly the adherence to necessary process.

- Some of those who grew the business during Fun and Whitewater may leave when the organization hits Predictable Success and a new culture of cross-functional decision making takes hold.

# [ CHAPTER SIX ]

## TREADMILL: WORKING HARD, GOING NOWHERE—THE OVERMANAGED ORGANIZATION

"This isn't about us getting bigger, faster. This is about us becoming better, faster."
—Mickey Drexler, former CEO, Gap, Inc.

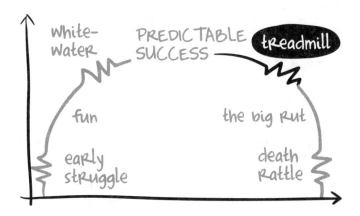

THE EMAIL WAS SHOCKING, BUT IT WASN'T A SURPRISE. I'D SENSED for almost six months that Derek was no longer happy, even though as CEO of a highly successful PR agency he'd been receiving more industry plaudits, more recognition and a higher income than ever before.

In our recent coaching sessions together, Derek had expressed an increasing degree of disillusionment and frustration, and despite the strong growth of his business, he personally seemed further and further removed from it and uncharacteristically directionless. His growing disengagement had in turn unsettled his lieutenants, and I'd begun to hear whispers of conflict—something I hadn't seen in the seven years I'd worked with the business.

So when I read his curt and strangely dispassionate email telling me that he had not only left the business, but also sold his remaining shares to the large advertising agency that had bought a majority interest thirteen months previously, it was with a mixture of relief and apprehension: relief that Derek had at least found a resolution—however drastic—to his discontentment, and apprehension for what his departure would mean for the business.

As the founder, Derek had always been the personification of his creative, visionary business. It had been his "baby" for many years, and he had molded the PR company in his likeness: bold, risk taking, entrepreneurial. After a few years of fast growth the business had inevitably hit Whitewater in a big way, and in response Derek had invested nearly three years in reinventing himself and the business. He learned to work less as an all-powerful founder/owner and more as the leader of a highly effective team, delegating responsibilities to his managers, developing them as individuals and as a team, and systematizing the organization's operations, while retaining the creativity and flexibility that his clients loved so much.

It wasn't long before the business moved into Predictable Success and became the regionally dominant player in its industry. With this success came visibility, recognition and more opportunities than Derek could exploit. After a swift courtship, he had sold first a minority, then a majority share in the business to a national advertising agency—a move that gave him access to unparalleled resources, the title of CEO and a seat on the advertising agency's board.

For a while, everything seemed rosy—the PR company continued along its upward trajectory and gradually integrated its operations into the parent company's systems. Just a few months in, however, I began to notice the change in Derek. He was becoming increasingly resentful of the increased oversight of his day-to-day activities, and he found it particularly hard to cope when several of his ideas were vetoed by the parent company's board. It seemed to him that his company was losing its edge—the rainmakers weren't bringing in the type of new work his company had previously won, and the client account managers seemed to emphasize process over creativity.

I'd watched as Derek increasingly sought forgiveness rather than permission for his actions, and I grimaced as I saw him try to function outside of the very systems with which he had worked so hard to align the company. Recently, it had almost seemed as if a cold war had opened up between Derek and a couple of his loyal staffers, and the rest of the organization.

Now this. He'd gone, left his baby "unilaterally, and with immediate effect," in the stilted prose of his email. I looked at the phone . . . this would be a hard call to make.

# Hearing What You Want to Hear

Derek's home office was a shrine to his considerable accomplishments—pictures of Derek with the movers and shakers in his industry, certificates and awards on the walls and on his credenza, tchotchkes and gifts from deliriously happy clients, and framed copies of headlines, column inches, magazine covers and TV appearances he had obtained for his clients over the years. In the middle of all this, Derek sat behind a desk covered with papers, reports and printouts, for all the world still the captain of a major company with hundreds of staff.

After receiving his email, I'd called Derek. He was clearly reluctant to talk, and I had to cash in some of my chips from our long relationship to insist that he let me come visit him. His hooded, downcast eyes barely made contact with mine. "There isn't much to talk about," he said. "It didn't work out. Period." I let the silence hang in the air. I knew Derek well enough to know that there *was* much to talk about—I just needed to let him do so in his own time. In his own way.

After a minute or so, Derek looked up at me. "Look," he said, "they changed the whole place beyond recognition. Turned it into a bean-counter's paradise. I couldn't get a thing done without filling in twenty forms and waiting three weeks for an answer from on high." He looked up at the ceiling and swiveled his feet up onto the desk. "Our work was crap. The client execs were so busy attending meetings and generating reports that they couldn't produce diddly-squat." He sighed, and relit the cigar he'd been pulling on. "We started losing clients—I haven't lost a client because of poor work since . . . you know . . . ." He looked up at me again.

"Whitewater . . . ?" I said.

Derek grimaced. "Yeah . . . Whitewater. Don't get me started. I thought when we invested all that time and energy getting out of Whitewater that we'd got this thing licked. I thought we were unbeatable. Then this happens." Derek's face clouded, his cheeks visibly flushed. It was clear he was angry, and part of that anger was directed at me. "You told me we'd reached Predictable Success—you told me we'd hit our prime. I believed you. Instead, I've lost everything. I'm starting all over again—at forty-seven!"

This was tough. It was hard not to get defensive—to remind Derek of our many discussions about what might happen if he sold an interest in his business to a bigger firm, to replay some of our long, late-night telephone conversations about the dangers of oversystematizing his business. Most of all, it was hard not to pull out my notes from our coaching sessions, when I had implored Derek to begin the process of institutionalizing the vision, creativity and entrepreneurial zeal that he personally represented, and that the company badly needed in all parts of its operations.

Yet despite my desire to post-rationalize, it was clear that I had failed Derek. Somehow, in the many hours we'd spent together, I had failed to get across to him the dangers of sliding from Predictable Success to Treadmill. Now, there was little I could do to help, except listen and give Derek a chance to work through his grief.

"Where do you think it went wrong?" I asked. "What could you have done differently?"

Derek swung his legs off the desk, stood up, and strolled to the French doors that opened from his home office to the pool and patio where his two kids played outside. He looked at them for a long time, deep in thought.

Twice, Derek tried to start a sentence but trailed off. "Nuthin' you didn't warn me about," he said eventually.

"I remember you warning me that the acquisition would have its pros and cons. You told me it would accelerate our growth both positively and negatively. I remember that." He turned and looked at me from across the room. "I guess I only really wanted to hear the good stuff." Derek gestured back toward his children in the distance. "Sometimes, you only want to hear the good stuff."

I smiled wanly. "I have three kids, too," I said. "I understand."

Derek came back to the desk, sat down and grabbed a pen from an ornate marble penholder. "It wasn't all their fault," he said, opening a plush leather folder. "They"—I assumed he was talking about the company that had taken over his—"sure made some mistakes, but I didn't react real well. I started this business because I wanted freedom to do my own thing, and the more I felt I was losing that freedom, the more I squirmed. Eventually, I had to get out." As Derek began to write something in his folder, I suspected he was moving out of grief and into something more positive.

He continued to talk as he scribbled. "I'll be okay—I did pretty well out of the sale of my shares, and I've a couple of other irons in the fire that I'm gonna pursue. In fact, I'm kinda excited"—Derek looked up at me and smiled for the first time since I'd arrived—"truth be told, I haven't felt this excited since I first started the business all those years ago." He looked down at his folder and began writing again.

"The key thing now is for you to help the business get back to Predictable Success. They can do it without me—in fact, it'll be better for them if they do it without me. But the key thing is this: they"—by now, we both knew who "they" were—"need to acknowledge the fact that the business ain't in Predictable Success anymore." Derek stopped writing and turned his folder round so I could see what he had written. It was a list of maybe eight or nine things.

"These are the processes they implemented—the most important ones—that are strangling the company. This stuff is squeezing the lifeblood out of everyone, killing any chance of doing quality work and genuinely growing the business." Derek looked at me intently. "You need to help them fix this. Help them get out of . . . what was it? You had a word for it . . . ?"

"Treadmill . . . ," I said, musing. "Treadmill."

# What Treadmill Is

Treadmill is the fifth stage in any organization's development, coming after Early Struggle, Fun, Whitewater and Predictable Success.

An organization moves into Treadmill whenever it becomes over-dependent on the systems and processes it implemented during White-water to push the organization into Predictable Success—in other words, the organization becomes oversystematized.

While technically there is no reason this must happen—in theory, an organization can remain in Predictable Success indefinitely—in practice, the slide forward into Treadmill happens for understandable, if unfortunate, reasons. After all, if the systemization that got us into Predictable Success is a good thing, then why not have more of it? If processes help us restabilize and grow our business anew, then surely the more, the better?

But of course, that isn't the case. Too many systems and processes in an organization cause it to slow down and lose its flexibility, and lead it to look inward rather than outward. The oversystematized organization becomes sclerotic, robotic and slow to react. Getting things done becomes tortuous and laborious, and perfectly good decisions about strategy and tactics increasingly are left unimplemented. This is not because the decisions themselves are poor (that will come later, as the organization slides into The Big Rut), but because there isn't the will or the ability to overcome the considerable difficulties in getting decisions translated into quick action.

Form-filling and statistical analysis begin to overtake productivity and output in importance. Management, while still overtly calling for growth and productivity, is increasingly more concerned with *how* something is done rather than *what* is being done. Form begins to usurp function: Is the right checklist being completed? Is the right flowchart being followed? Are "The Three Steps to . . ." or "The Five Elements of . . ." being correctly implemented?

In the Treadmill organization, incremental efficiencies become paramount—useful tools such as Kaizen, Six Sigma or Continuous Improvement are raised to the status of dogma, and the honing and perfection of process becomes a valued skill. Compliance with process becomes mandatory, and for the first time a policing function emerges, tasked with finding and eradicating noncompliance.

## The Loss of "Wow!"

Very quickly, the oversystematized organization begins to lose the vision and entrepreneurial zeal that was previously its competitive advantage.

When the organization is in Predictable Success, systems and process act as a benevolent protector of creativity and risk taking, providing rules and boundaries for the organization's vision and entrepreneurial zeal to flourish. All the while these systems also act as a counterbalance to chaos and caprice—the unpredictable by-products of creativity and risk taking that were so prevalent in Fun.

Figure 6.1 Systems and Process in Predictable Success

In Treadmill, systems and process turn inward, and instead of protecting creativity and risk taking begin, like a malevolent creature in a bad horror movie, to wrap their tendrils around the organization's vision and entrepreneurial zeal, and slowly choke it to death.

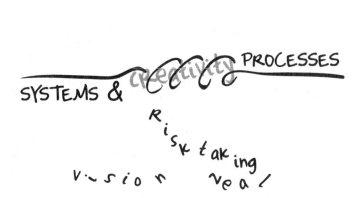

Figure 6.2 Systems and Process in Treadmill

The slow choking of creativity and risk taking during Treadmill has many effects on the organization, but three are particularly impactful:

**1. The loss of innovation.** In Treadmill, it becomes easier to copy than innovate. As the tendrils of systems and processes choke the organization's vision and entrepreneurial zeal, "best practices" and "benchmarking" replace creativity and risk taking. New ideas are frowned upon (because they disrupt the incumbent systems and processes), and instead the organization imports the practices and ideas of other, similar organizations—that is, organizations with similar systems and processes, and hence, organizations that are similarly in Treadmill.

**2. The loss of "step growth."** While an organization is in Predictable Success, in addition to steady incremental growth, the active culture of creativity and risk taking in the organization delivers periodic, substantial growth spurts—"step growth" caused by innovation in technology, sales or marketing. In Predictable Success, the organization is also able to use such "step" changes to respond transformationally to challenges it faces, such as the rise of a major new competitor or the development of a competing technology.

In Treadmill, as we've seen, the ability to innovate is lost, replaced by imitation. Taken together, this loss of innovation, the sheer complexity of getting things done, the loss of creativity and risk taking, and the relentless focus on iterative, incremental change mean that it becomes almost impossible for the business to deliver significant step growth. Even when faced with an external challenge, the organization in Treadmill cannot respond transformationally and must instead endeavor to make its way out incrementally of the situation.

**3. The suppression of bad news.** When an organization is in Treadmill, compliance with process becomes absolute. The budgetary process is no exception—in fact, it is often the most prominent process for which compliance is required: "Hitting the numbers" is not optional, and a culture develops of "don't bring me any surprises."

Not surprisingly, as a result, "surprises" (anything that is a deviation from the norm, a negative result or bad news of any sort) are suppressed. If you've been told not to bring bad news, well . . . you don't bring bad news. As we'll see shortly, this symptom of Treadmill is highly dangerous; if not corrected it will be the leading cause of the organization's further decline into The Big Rut.

Taken together, these attributes doom the organization to mere mediocrity. No longer is it capable of the "Wow!" effect—it can no longer achieve anything spectacular or thrilling, can no longer post double-digit growth as a result of controlled innovation and risk taking. Instead, it works and works its systems, polishing and burnishing incremental improvements, eking out marginal growth, one painful, small step at a time.

# Working for an Organization in Treadmill

Working for an organization in Treadmill can be exceptionally frustrating for some people and bliss for others.

**Veterans**—those who have worked for the organization for some time— find it highly frustrating to see the organization slide into Treadmill. They balk at the oversystematization, resent the imposition of intrusive reporting processes and recoil at the micromanagement that accompanies both. Increasingly, they feel distanced from once-close management, sense that they are no longer trusted and feel "out of the loop."

For such veterans, there is often an almost laughable lack of reality in management's pronouncements—everything seems managed for effect, and the CYA culture that has developed means that there appears to be little truth-telling anymore. They leave staff meetings thinking, "That manager just spoke for thirty minutes and said nothing at all." The point-lessness of railing against the system becomes clear when one or two people are publicly demoted or fired for trying to buck the system, or for being too free with bad news or criticism.

**New employees,** on the other hand, enjoy working for the organization in Treadmill—at least for a while. Recruited for their ability (and desire) to work within proscribed systems, employees hired in Treadmill tend to be more rigid, systems-oriented individuals than the veterans, and thus fit in with—even thrive in—Treadmill. The hiring process in Treadmill empha-sizes teamwork, adherence to process, and conservatism above vision, cre-ativity and risk taking.

For such new employees, Treadmill can be a heaven to work in: sys-tems are well defined and adhered to, process is upheld, and there are few surprises. Resources are provided in order to get the job done, in return for which each employee is expected to account for his or her actions and to provide adequate and appropriate reports. If there isn't exactly a culture of challenge and debate, the employee may think, "Well, I get that in my sports, or at home, or in my social life. At work, I do what is asked of me, and I'm reasonably well looked after in return."

**For the founder or owner,** Treadmill is a make-or-break experience. Assuming they were able to undergo the personal transformation neces-sary to get through Whitewater and into Predictable Success, for most founder/owners, sliding into Treadmill is a traumatic experience.

Whether—as in Derek's case—the business has been bought out by a bigger parent or not, the organization in Treadmill loses its last vesti-gial elements of being a "family" or "small" business, and transforms into an impersonal machine. Coupled with the loss of personal freedom and autonomy that Treadmill brings, and the micromanaging, "looking over your shoulder" intrusiveness of the Treadmill culture, most founders and owners feel increasingly isolated and distant from what was once their "baby."

No longer recognizing this entity as their own, highly entrepreneurial founder/owners can become disengaged and frustrated to a dangerous degree. As the founder or owner watches what "they" are doing to what was "my" business, he or she can become bitter, even jealous. At its most extreme, this frustration and bitterness can lead a founder or owner to become a highly visible, negative influence within the organization, exercising obstructionism and factionalism to build a vociferous fifth column, railing against the new management style that has taken hold.

Not surprisingly, Treadmill is the stage at which most founders and owners eventually part company with the organization they created, either voluntarily, in a recognition that this business is no longer the one they created and no longer brings them fulfillment, or involuntarily, forced out in a coup headed by those who no longer feel comfortable with the highly visionary—as they now see it, disruptive—founder or owner.

# Getting Out of Treadmill

Treadmill is a dangerous stage for any organization to be in.

It is true that if managed correctly, the business is only one step away from moving back to Predictable Success. But if managed incorrectly, the organization will slide forward into The Big Rut, at which point it loses the power to self-diagnose its condition, and it will be locked into an inevitable decline into Death Rattle and oblivion.

In Chapter 10: What to Do When You've Overshot—Recovering From Treadmill, we explore in detail the precise technical steps required in order to bring an organization back from Treadmill to Predictable Success. But in order for management to take those steps, it must first *recognize the need to do so*. And it is here that the main danger lurks for the organization in Treadmill.

Just as we've seen in previous stages of development, such as Fun and Whitewater, it is rare that managers spend their time thinking, "What stage of organizational development are we in?" Instead, managers are simply going about their day-to-day business, trying to run a successful organization. Like the mythological frog in cold water, they don't notice the heat is being turned up one degree at a time. And just as the frog will remain in the pot until the heat reaches the point where it is boiled alive, so management continues on with its day-to-day activities, generally impervious to the changes that have taken it from Predictable Success to Treadmill.

Now, while we have seen this frog-boiling dynamic at work in previous stages of the organization's development, it is particularly dangerous in Treadmill because of something we saw earlier: *the suppression of bad news.*

Because Treadmill brings with it a CYA, comply-at-all-costs, bring-me-no-surprises culture, it becomes increasingly unacceptable to confront management with anything that smacks of bad news—including criticism of any sort. This precludes pointing out the loss of creativity, risk taking, innovation and vision that is threatening the organization's continued growth and development—that is, assuming anyone spots it in the first place.

The natural source of such bad news would normally be the founder/owner, but he or she either has already departed (didn't make the transition from Whitewater) or is increasingly seen as a disruptive and negative force whose views are interpreted as mere invective.

So how can an organization in Treadmill recognize the situation it is in, allowing it to implement the steps outlined in Chapter 10 and return to Predictable Success?

## 1. START WHILE STILL IN PREDICTABLE SUCCESS.

As we've seen numerous times, it is very hard for management to identify the movement of the organization from one stage in its life cycle to the next, except in retrospect. It is therefore important—*while the organization is still in Predictable Success*—to put "sensors" in place that will sound an alarm when there are indications that the organization may be sliding into Treadmill.

## 2. USE REAL PEOPLE.

It is tempting to make these sensors just another system or process—a report or checklist, say, or some sort of executive dashboard that somehow measures the organization's health. But remember, an overdependence on systems and processes is the very thing that we're trying to avoid. It is much better to use *real people* as our sensors—so long as they are truth-tellers, unafraid to say it as they see it, and have little or no reason to withhold bad news or avoid difficult conversations.

## 3. APPOINT ONE OR MORE NONEXECUTIVE BOARD MEMBERS.

The best spot to start placing Treadmill sensors is right at the top—on the company's board. There are many good reasons for appointing strong, nonexecutive directors on your board, and this is among the very best—they can help spot and arrest a slide into Treadmill.

For this to work effectively, the individuals chosen need to meet some minimum criteria:

- They should be able to hold their own with the senior management of the organization.
- They should be outspoken without being opinionated.
- They should ideally have worked previously with an organization that slid from Predictable Success to Treadmill and be able to recognize the signs.
- They should not be pals with or cronies of the CEO or any other member of senior management. In fact, the less they know of the organization and its people at the start, the better it will be.

## 4. GIVE YOUR TOP THREE EXECUTIVES AN EXTERNAL COACH.

An important indicator of whether or not the organization is sliding from Predictable Success into Treadmill is the way in which the organization's most senior executives conduct themselves, particularly in the degree to which they are outward-looking, visionary, creative and risk taking, as

opposed to inward-looking and conservative. Allowing for natural varia-
tions between individuals, by and large, as the organization begins to
slide toward Treadmill, its senior executives tend to become more insular and conservative, exchanging time formerly spent experimenting and
exchanging and developing knowledge for time spent on data analysis
and process enforcement.

One effective way to both prevent and monitor such a change is to
appoint external coaches to work with at least the top three senior executives in the organization. The coaches should possess the same characteristics as the external board members detailed above (but should not be the
same people—these are two distinct roles, and it fatally weakens each to
mix them).

## 5. HOLD A BIANNUAL "ADVANCE."

Most organizations that reach Predictable Success regularly hold some
sort of executive retreat, typically structured to allow senior management
to spend time on the organization's medium- and long-term strategy. An
"advance" is the opposite of a retreat—it focuses on everything *but* the
organization, instead concentrating only on the external environment in
which the organization operates: the overall industry, its main competitors, its supply chain, and technological, legislative, environmental and
socio-economic changes.

The "advance," of course, complements the "retreat" by informing the
development of the organization's own strategy. By precluding any immediate consideration of the internal impact on the organization during the
"advance," however, it also forces management to remain outward-looking, to think creatively about the environment within which it operates,
and to be honest in its assessment of external threats and opportunities
faced by the organization.

## 6. ENFORCE MBWA.

Tom Peters' ground-breaking 1982 book *In Search of Excellence* has suf-
fered major revisionism over the years since, particularly after many of

his so-called excellent companies stumbled, or in some cases outright failed (an eventuality, incidentally, from which Peters never claimed they were exempt). One concept he introduced has remained unscarred and is a powerful tool in the battle to prevent the slide from Predictable Success to Treadmill: "management by walking around" (MBWA).

In practical terms, this means enforcing a minimum degree of unstructured face-to-face contact between managers and their direct reports, peers and line managers. Simple as that. An organization that is sliding toward Treadmill will display an undue use of technology (voicemail, email, video-conferencing, intranet, extranet and social media) not just as a vehicle for communication, but increasingly as a way to avoid real, genuine communication.

It's rather like the difference between buying a book or a pair of shoes online, and going to a bookstore or department store: There are times (particularly when you know precisely what you want) when the online experience is unbeatable, but there are also occasions in which the browsing experience of a physical store is needed to provide the range of options, side-by-side comparison and plain capriciousness that are much harder to replicate online.

Similarly, the organization in Predictable Success discovers nuggets and gems in the sidebars of unplanned, unstructured face-to-face discussion, while the organization that is sliding toward Treadmill begins to squeeze out such interactions, deeming them unnecessary and perhaps even unwanted (because such interaction doesn't easily sit with systems and processes).

## 7. START AN INTERNAL MENTORING PROGRAM.

The best people to act as effective Treadmill sensors are your own employees—provided they can speak honestly and without retribution in a risk-free environment. The best way to produce such an environment is to start an internal mentoring program in which the mentors are not from the mentees' department or team, thus freeing both participants from the constraints of direct-line responsibility. Such a program—focusing on the development of the individual, not on his or her core skills—if maintained over time rather than as a one-off "initiative," develops strong internal lines of honest communication that in turn provide a healthy reality check on whether or not the organization is indeed drifting toward Treadmill.

## 8. ENCOURAGE (AND USE) SABBATICALS, JOB-SHARING AND EMPLOYEE EXCHANGES.

It will be clear by now that one of the key dynamic forces that pushes an organization out of Predictable Success and into Treadmill is that of *insularity*. Management begins to spend more and more time focusing inward, polishing systems and processes, enforcing compliance and consistency, and eschewing time spent investigating, researching and experimenting from first principles. One indicator of this trend is the amount of time senior executives spend *not* working on their key responsibilities.

This may seem counterintuitive—Isn't the CIO there to manage the organization's information needs? Isn't the CFO there to manage the finances?—but the fact is that the healthy organization in Predictable Success stays there by exposing itself, through its executives, to other experiences, other realities, other solutions, other questions, other answers. In Treadmill, the organization begins to lose the ability to *learn*, as curiosity is replaced by the need for affirmation, experimentation is replaced by mere copying, and trial and error is replaced by mandate.

To prevent the onset of this slow ossification, encourage (and take, yourself) regular sabbaticals. Allow executives to job-share with others. Consider temporary job exchanges where one or more of your executives trade places with a peer from your supply chain, a major customer or even another industry. This simple exposure to other voices and other eyes acts like an open window to the outside world, bringing fresh and ever-changing noises, smells and experiences into the organization, and in itself acting as a strong bulwark to the onset of Treadmill.

## SUMMARY

- Treadmill is the fifth stage in any organization's development, coming after Early Struggle, Fun, Whitewater and Predictable Success.

- An organization moves into Treadmill when it becomes overdependent on systems and processes.

- Oversystemization in turn leads to a loss of creativity, risk taking and entrepreneurial zeal.

- This can often be accompanied by the departure of the founder or owner, as he or she becomes frustrated, loses autonomy and seeks new challenges.

- Treadmill is not inevitable—an organization can avoid it (and stay in Predictable Success) by "institutionalizing" creativity, risk taking and entrepreneurial zeal.

- When in Treadmill, it is possible to step back into Predictable Success by reintroducing creativity, risk taking and entrepreneurial zeal.

- If the organization does not do so, it will decline further, sliding into The Big Rut.

- The key difference between Treadmill and The Big Rut is that in Treadmill the organization is still capable of self-diagnosis, and can therefore correct its decline. In The Big Rut, the organization loses the ability to be self-diagnostic.

- Working for an organization in Treadmill can feel sterile and unfulfilling. There is a preference for form over function, and compliance over results.

# [ CHAPTER SEVEN ]

## THE BIG RUT: IN THE ORGANIZATIONAL COMFORT ZONE—REARRANGING THE DECK CHAIRS

"If anything ever happens around here, we're ready for it."
—Anonymous

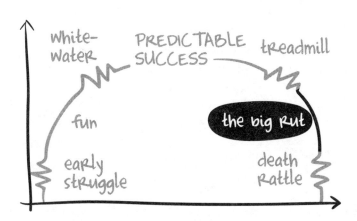

IT WAS THE SECOND TIME IN MY CAREER THAT I'D BEEN LED TO A client's premises by my nose. Once, years previously, I'd had the doubtful pleasure of auditing the books of a massive tire manufacturer, and the smell of rubber had seemingly lingered for months. Now, it was a somewhat more pleasurable olfactory experience, but even more marked: chocolate. It was dense in the air, unmistakable, heady and (in those pre-GPS days) a highly effective trail that led me straight to the premises of the candy manufacturer I was here to see.

I guessed the inhabitants of this small town in northern England had gotten used to it over the years, but to a new visitor the pervasive odor, together with the dominating shape of the candy manufacturer's processing plant and offices, gave the whole place the sense of a "factory town." Street after street of what I supposed had once been workers' tenement houses radiated outward from the factory, and the name of the family that owned the company was apparent everywhere—street names, a couple of schools and the town's small hospital all bore witness to the benefaction of the same family.

I pulled into the large but strangely unpopulated parking lot, and stepped out of the car to be confronted by an imposing granite building of Dickensian proportions. The whole of the front facade was a monument to dour industry—window after window of small leaded lights, behind which I assumed lay both the manufacturing plant and the administrative offices.

I walked toward the sculpted archway in front, with its massive double doors. As I reached for the ornate ironwork door-handle, which was the size of a man's head, I saw a sheet of paper taped at eye level behind a rain-spattered protective sheet: "Visitors, please use the side entrance. Deliveries to the rear." The main doors, splendid as they were, looked as though they hadn't been opened for decades.

# Echoes and Nods

Twenty minutes later, I was sitting in an anteroom adjacent to what appeared to be a massive dining hall, waiting to see the three family scions that a mutual friend had recommended I meet with. From what I knew, this once nationally loved business had over many decades shrunk to its current position of having just two products—an eponymously named chocolate bar and a strangely shaped circular confection—that were very popular with an aging demographic. I knew from personal experience that these products were hard to find and—even if you did find somewhere that stocked them—were inconsistently available. They were the type of confection that my mother would have regularly brought home when I was a child, but in my adult life they had become drowned out by the wall-to-wall marketing and distribution of the major multinational confectionary companies.

"Pleased to meet you, I'm sure." The voice startled me—I hadn't heard anyone come into the anteroom. As I looked up and stood in the same motion, I saw that the door to the dining hall was open, and I was being beckoned in by a tall patrician gentleman in a heavy, wool, three-piece suit. Behind him, at what seemed to be an aircraft carrier's distance away, two other equally formal-looking individuals, one male, one female, sat behind a massive boardroom table. It became clear that the "dining hall" was actually the largest, oldest and most formal boardroom I'd ever seen.

"Do take a seat. Make yourself at home." I was motioned to a tall upright chair at one end of the highly polished, never-ending table. My host took a seat beside what I assumed to be his brother and sister—at the far end of the table. Were we going to use semaphore flags to communicate?

In fact, sound traveled very well—albeit by echo—in this wood-floored, granite-walled mausoleum. "Did you have a pleasant journey?" boomed the senior brother. "Yes," I replied. My voice sounded like a squeak in the resonating auditorium. "Very nice, thank you." For some reason, it felt as if I was visiting with an aunt and uncles I didn't know very well, but with whom I had to be on my best behavior.

"Very good. Now, James"—James was the company's financial advisor and our mutual contact—". . . James tells us that you are a bright young man with clever ideas about business." I couldn't think of much to say to this remark, so I responded with a smile and what I hoped was a diffident nod of my head. "Very good," he continued, "James speaks very highly of you. He . . . uhm . . ." At this, the elder brother seemed to lose interest in finishing the sentence. He looked from side to side at his siblings, eyebrows raised, rather hoping they might finish the thought for him.

Eventually, the younger sister chimed in. "James thought we might benefit from meeting with you?" She phrased it as a question, her voice going up at the end of the sentence. She shook her head slightly from side to side as she said it, as if the suggestion was mildly bewildering. I was getting confused. Perhaps I had got the wrong end of the stick.

I said, "My understanding from James is that you are facing some problems in growing your business. I understood from him you are looking for ways in which to revive your brand and rejuvenate your customer base. He thought perhaps I might be able to help you with that . . ." The body language coming from across the table cut me short. The sister and elder brother sat erect and unmoving, looking at me rather as if I were trying to explain a complex quadratic equation. The only facial reaction I could see came from the younger brother, who was slowly stirring the contents of a porcelain teacup, one eyebrow raised and with a disdainful smirk on his face. I thought it best to remain silent.

Eventually, the younger brother looked up at me long enough to let his tea settle. "James has . . . how shall I put it . . . a tendency to overdramatize." He looked to each of his siblings as if for affirmation. "I don't think we require anything quite of the nature you describe." The smallest of nods from the other two indicated that they were all in agreement with this.

## Here Since 1908

The next twenty minutes were excruciating, as I tried to clarify just what position their business was in, how I might help them and whether, in fact, they really wanted any help in the first place. Were they experiencing a decline in market share? "We sell everything we produce." Did they have problems in sustaining consistent distribution? "Our wholesalers take what we deliver to them without complaint." Were they concerned about the aging demographic of their end consumer? "We've been selling our products since 1908." Was there a threat of being totally eclipsed by the major confectionery manufacturers? "We've been selling our products since 1908." I felt like a prosecutor cross-examining a witness for the defense. A hostile witness, at that.

Finally, there was only one question left. "Is there anything whatsoever you think I could help you with?" I asked, trying to keep the increasing sense of frustration I felt out of my voice. The three siblings embarked on their now familiar routine of first staring into space, then slowly, and indirectly at one another. I waited to see which of them might deign to respond to my importunate question.

Finally, the eldest brother bowed to the responsibility of seniority and answered. "I think not. But thank you so much for popping along. This has been a most enlightening and enjoyable discussion." I looked at him, trying to detect even a hint of irony in his tone, but there was none.

As I gathered my things to leave, the eldest brother stood to escort me out. We walked to the boardroom door. I couldn't contain myself. Before leaving, there was something I needed to know. "Tell me one thing," I said, turning to include the others in my question. "If everything in the business is as good as you say it is, why did you agree to meet with me in the first place?"

This time it was the sister who volunteered an answer. "Gosh, every business gets itself into a little rut from time to time, doesn't it? We thought it would be nice to talk to someone with an outside perspective—see if we're still doing the right things, you know? And I think we can agree, our little chat has done just that." She looked to the others, and received the required nod of assent.

As I stood outside unlocking my car, I looked back at the dank building—it was raining by now, adding an even darker hue to the landscape—and an important realization came to me. Yes, the sister had been right: Every organization "gets itself into a little rut from time to time." I'd seen it happen even to organizations in Predictable Success. But this was different. What this company was experiencing wasn't a "little rut" on the way to success—they had entered an entire stage of development all its own, and a very dangerous one. This business was in what I would in time come to call "The *Big* Rut."

## What The Big Rut Is

The Big Rut is the sixth and penultimate stage in any organization's development, coming after Early Struggle, Fun, Whitewater, Predictable Success and Treadmill.

Once it reaches this stage in development, the organization has lost any desire to be creative or take risks, and is instead solely focused on maintaining and marginally improving how it has done business in the past. When in The Big Rut, there is a belief on the part of management that "the way we've always done things" is the main contributing factor to the organization's success, and that changes should not be made to existing formulae, systems and processes.

The key focus of the organization in The Big Rut is itself, not the customer. Customers are viewed as distractions at worst, and at best as uninformed and in need of being told what's best for them. Internal matters, such as job titles, car parking spaces, size of offices and management perks, are all viewed as having more importance than pleasing the customer.

Organizations in The Big Rut tend to have a paternalistic—even at times condescending—attitude toward both customers and suppliers, and as they often have a monopolistic position in their markets (or at least have a strong balance sheet), they can afford to maintain such an attitude with impunity—at least until the money runs out.

# How Organizations Fall into The Big Rut

Although it is by far the most dangerous stage in any organization's development (because once there, descent into Death Rattle is all but inevitable), falling into The Big Rut happens with deceptive ease: It's a result simply of staying in Treadmill. Hang around in Treadmill for too long, and a number of important changes begin to occur that, taken together, push the organization into The Big Rut:

**1. Key personnel leave.** When the organization first moves from Predictable Success to Treadmill, it takes with it all the key personnel who have together built the organization's success. This includes the visionary risk takers and creative zealots as well as the administrators and systematizers, who together developed the delicate balance required in Predictable Success.

As Treadmill progresses, the first people to get frustrated are the more entrepreneurial, creative and risk taking types; the administrators and systematizers are less disturbed by the impact of Treadmill. If Treadmill continues for any length of time (certainly more than a year), the more entrepreneurial people in the organization begin to leave, taking with them the organization's ability to be (and interest in being) creative and visionary. As we've already seen, this can often include the original founder/owners, if they haven't left or been replaced already.

**2. Creativity, risk taking, vision and zeal all die.** Eventually, all the creativity and vision are squeezed out of the organization. Initiative and risk taking are actively discouraged, and compliance and consistency are rewarded. Decision making becomes a lengthy, tortuous, formulaic process, and as a result, apart from the annual budgeting process, most people elect to avoid anything that will involve extracting a decision from management.

Developing anything new, such as strategies, products or marketing programs, is almost unheard of, and innovation is restricted to the late adoption of only those technological or other changes that have been definitively proven in the marketplace.

As a result, an organization in The Big Rut consistently lags some years behind its competitors.

**3. Interest in the customer is replaced by navel-gazing.** As the organization loses interest in innovation and risk taking, it also loses its original vision, which in turn leads to a loss of interest in the customer. In this regard, the organization in The Big Rut becomes an almost exact mirror image of what it was in Fun: In Fun, the organization is completely focused externally, on the customer's needs, to the detriment of its internal systems. In The Big Rut, the organization becomes focused on its own internal needs, to the almost total exclusion of any real interest in the customer.

Of course, the organization in The Big Rut, having taken some time to get there and having been through all the preceding stages of development, will almost certainly have a marketing department, maybe even a

PR department, and a customer service department. And over time, the organization will have learned how to pay lip service to the customer, making all the right noises about "customer focus" and being "forward-facing." But internally, the customer is disregarded, in some cases even despised as an inconvenient irritation to the daily business of "doing what we did before."

**4. Frustration is replaced by complacency.** In Treadmill, the organization's salvation lies in the frustration of senior managers who want to change the direction in which the organization is going—to reverse course and return to Predictable Success. In The Big Rut, management becomes comfortable with where the organization is headed, happy with their lot in life and complacent about the future. It is this complacency that defines The Big Rut and that makes the next stage—a slide into Death Rattle and oblivion—almost inevitable.

## The Roots of Complacency

Getting out of The Big Rut is exceptionally rare. Most organizations that fall into it never get out—in almost every case, an organization's last hope for salvation is in Treadmill.

As we've seen, the main reason for this is in the complacency with which management views the situation. They either cannot—or don't want to—see the dire straits the company is in. There can be several root causes for this:

**1. The organization has a monopolistic market share.** If an organization has an exceptional run in Predictable Success, it can build itself to the position where it develops a monopoly—or near-monopoly—in its market. When this happens, lack of competition will eventually result in the development of the complacency that pushes the organization into The Big Rut. In this example, the transition through Treadmill can often be very short, with the organization moving from Predictable Success into The Big Rut relatively quickly.

**2. The company is cash rich.** Even without a monopoly, the organization may well have taken some time—maybe decades—to get into Treadmill, during which time it will have built up considerable reserves, providing a "cash cushion" that insulates the organization from the impact of its actions. When this happens, executives can afford to become complacent, as there is no immediate feedback that tells them they may be endangering their company.

**3. The senior executives are disproportionately remunerated.** Often accompanying one or more of the first two examples (enjoying a monopoly and/or being cash rich), there is an additional factor: The senior executives are simply so well paid to maintain the status quo that they have little incentive to change anything or to rock the boat by proposing anything radical.

This situation is most likely to occur either when the senior management is distinct and distant from ownership (such as in publicly held companies, NGOs and not-for-profits), thus removing any effective oversight of executive pay and reducing the likelihood of any investigation into whether the organization is receiving value for money in executive compensation, or in tightly held family companies where ownership and management are the same, resulting again in a lack of independent oversight.

**4. It is a family business in the second (or later) generation.** Sometimes an organization falls into The Big Rut simply because the owners don't know what to do with the business. Particularly with family companies that refuse to look outside for management help, simple generational transference can produce the complacency required to push them from Treadmill into The Big Rut.

A common pattern is as follows: The first generation, visionary and entrepreneurial, build the organization and take it to the top of Fun—or, if they're lucky and hard-working, briefly into Predictable Success. The second generation, somewhat less visionary, nonetheless grasp the opportunity to build on their parents' success, and implement the systems and processes needed to push into and stay in Predictable Success. The third generation, knowing only systems and processes, simply "rinse and repeat" what has gone before, driving the business through Treadmill and into The Big Rut.

(Of course, there are many examples of the opposite occurring, with a son, daughter or grandchild rejuvenating a previously moribund business and taking it to new heights and back to Predictable Success, but statistically this is less common.)

# Getting Out of The Big Rut

As we've seen, getting out of The Big Rut is a difficult and rare occurrence. Generally speaking, when an organization does manage to shake itself out of its complacency and make the enormous changes needed to claw its way back to Treadmill, and thus to Predictable Success, it is a result of the organizational equivalent of a powerful slap in the face such as one might administer to a hysterical individual.

Here are the most common sources of such a powerful intervention:

**Acquisition.** Organizations in The Big Rut are often attractive acquisition targets—ironically for the very same reasons that got them there in the first place: a monopoly in their market, a cash-rich balance sheet and/or overpaid executives (providing a large opportunity for cost saving by installing new management at more realistic compensation levels).

Buying over an organization that is in The Big Rut, replacing management and rejuvenating the organization from top to bottom is the most common way to administer a sharp shock to the system and prevent a descent into Death Rattle.

Note that to succeed in this, it is vital that the acquirer purchase at least a majority share in the organization (100 percent is even better). This is because otherwise the enormous inertia inherent in the business will almost always prevent the required changes from taking place, and the acquirer will eventually lose the investment, with the company left just as firmly stuck in The Big Rut as before.

**Pending immediate collapse.** Very occasionally, an organization will face the prospect of a catastrophic immediate collapse that is so obvious and so potentially devastating, it will shake management (or the owners, who will in turn shake management) out of complacency. The most common example is a technological or legislative change that threatens to alter the competitive landscape so completely that even the organization's most complacent executives can see the writing on the wall—for example, the legislative changes in the 1980s that so galvanized the tobacco industry.

**The lucky noodle.** Even more rare—but fun when it happens—is when someone in the organization is breaking all the rules in a dark basement somewhere, and comes up with a product or service so obviously compelling that it reignites a sense of vision and zeal within the organization. While ninety-nine times out of a hundred this process will result simply in the errant individual "getting the boot" for such a brazen act of creativity, once in a while the result will be so irresistible as to sway even the most complacent management team into renewed action.

**Massive, overwhelming, authoritative imposition.** Most common in family companies (but not unheard of in public companies), this rarest of all interventions is when someone with the necessary power and authority simply receives a wake-up call and decides to take the organization by the scruff of the neck and turn it around, either directly themselves or indirectly by proxy.

While it is rare that this type of intervention actually happens, it is even less common for it to succeed—simply because the enormous degree of entropy in any organization that has fallen into The Big Rut can sandbag relatively easily any attempts to reverse direction. An individual seeking to change an organization in The Big Rut needs enormous resources (at least enough management talent at hand to remove most or all of the existing senior management), power, authority—and patience.

## SUMMARY

- The Big Rut is the sixth and penultimate stage in any organization's development, coming after Early Struggle, Fun, Whitewater, Predictable Success and Treadmill.

- An organization falls into The Big Rut when it ceases to see the customer as its main reason for being.

- Most organizations in The Big Rut view their own existence as their primary reason for being—in other words, they become self-perpetuating institutions.

- Organizations in The Big Rut are almost exclusively peopled with bureaucrats and administrators. Visionaries and hands-on operators leave in frustration.

- The difference between being in Treadmill and being in The Big Rut is that in Treadmill there is frustration with the organization's loss of creativity and vision. In The Big Rut creativity and vision are actively discouraged.

- When an organization falls into The Big Rut, it loses the ability to self-diagnose its condition. Only a massive external intervention can keep the organization from the final stage—Death Rattle.

- Organizations in The Big Rut are often cash rich and/or have a monopolistic hold on their market, so their inexorable decline can take a very long time.

- Working for an organization in The Big Rut is rewarding for bureaucratically minded individuals. Results-focused individuals tend not to stay around.

# [ CHAPTER EIGHT ]

## DEATH RATTLE: GOING QUIETLY INTO THAT GOOD NIGHT

"If you're killed, you've lost a very important part of your life."
—Brooke Shields

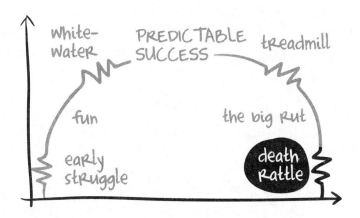

THERE'S NOTHING PRETTY, AND VERY LITTLE THAT'S INSTRUCTIVE, about watching an organization in the final stage of Death Rattle. I say this as a result of having witnessed the process many times, including twice in gruesome, intimate detail, with businesses of my own.

So I propose we linger only briefly on our examination of Death Rattle, not least because at this point, it is too late to do anything that might change the organization's fate—everything that could have happened to prevent the organization from sliding into oblivion should have happened long before now, possibly (though unlikely) in The Big Rut, and more probably in Treadmill.

## Then We Came to the End

No matter how well funded an organization is, how monopolistic its hold on the market is or how well paid its executives are, sooner or later, time will run out for an organization in The Big Rut. It may happen within months or it may take some time (I know of one educational establishment that has been in The Big Rut for almost one hundred years), but absent the type of violent intervention detailed in the previous chapter, at some point one of the following will happen to the organization:

**It will run out of resources.** The single most common reason for sliding from The Big Rut into Death Rattle is that the organization simply runs out of resources—usually cash. Over time the inattention to customers makes it harder and harder to sell the company's products or services, and lacking the ability to innovate, management does the only thing it knows how to do—drops its prices. And while this brings a temporary respite, it does so at the expense of profits.

Eventually demand slumps again, and management has to engage in another round of price cuts, repeating the process until finally the coffers are drained, leaving no option but to shut up shop.

**It will become technologically irrelevant.** As management is unwilling to engage in risky technological change, always waiting until any new technology is firmly entrenched in the industry before deciding to adopt it, the organization risks being made obsolete by rapid technological change—as happened, for example, to the companies that made audio cassettes and associated accessories and that failed to embrace the introduction of CD and DVD technology.

**The market will move away.** Customers don't like being ignored, and no matter how deep your pockets, if you ignore your customers for long enough, they will eventually go elsewhere, no matter how good you believe your product is. The US auto industry committed this cardinal sin throughout the 1970s and 1980s, paving the way for the rapid rise of imported motor vehicles and the eventual eclipse of the industry.

## Take Your Pick

As the organization's options slowly run out, eventually Death Rattle takes hold, and after a brief paroxysm of frenzied activity (lawyers are called, turnaround agents are fruitlessly consulted, bankers issue ultimata and fresh cash reserves are frantically sought) the organization ceases to exist in any meaningful way.

Technically, this usually happens through one of the following:

**A fire sale of the company.** This is not to be confused with the life-saving acquisition discussed in The Big Rut. Here there is no question of the organization surviving—this is merely a face-saving exercise on behalf of management, with maybe a few pennies on the dollar rescued for owners.

**Liquidation through bankruptcy.** This is a legal process that puts the organization out of its misery, often combined with the fire sale mentioned above. Again, this is not to be confused with bankruptcy in The Big Rut, which is used (in the US through the Chapter 11 process) to facilitate sweeping institutional change, and from which a rejuvenated company is expected to emerge. In Death Rattle, the bankruptcy (in the US known as Chapter 7) has no transformational powers and merely performs the necessary legal last rites over the dying company.

## SUMMARY

- Death Rattle is the seventh and final stage of an organization's development, coming after Early Struggle, Fun, Whitewater, Predictable Success, Treadmill and The Big Rut.

- It occurs at the end of The Big Rut, when the organization finally runs out of resources and/or its market disappears because of technological or other change, or simply because the organization is no longer meeting its customers' needs.

- Death Rattle usually takes the form of either a fire sale of the company's assets (perhaps including its brand name) or liquidation through bankruptcy.

# [ PART 2 ]

## ARRIVAL: GETTING TO PREDICTABLE SUCCESS—
## AND STAYING THERE

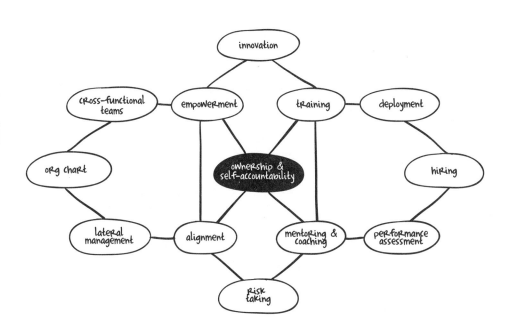

## CHAPTER NINE

## ALMOST THERE: BREAKING THROUGH WHITEWATER INTO PREDICTABLE SUCCESS

"The only way to change people's minds is with consistency."
—Jack Welch

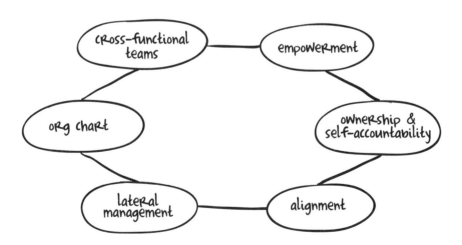

AS WE'VE SEEN IN PART I, AN ORGANIZATION WILL MOVE FROM Whitewater into Predictable Success only when management recognizes (and acts on) the need to implement those systems and processes that will enable the organization to first stabilize, then scale its operations efficiently.

But which systems and processes should management focus on? Faced with the tangled complexity of an organization in Whitewater, where is it best to begin? Which systems and processes will most accelerate the path from Whitewater to Predictable Success? Equally importantly, how does an organization know when to stop, in order to avoid pushing too far and moving into Treadmill?

Obviously, every organization is different, and so the answers to each of these questions to some extent varies from organization to organization. In each organization trying to move from Whitewater into Predictable Success, there will be some obvious "low-hanging fruit"—systems and processes that are obviously and immediately needed, and that are specific to the organization: say, an inventory control system or a product delivery tracking mechanism for one organization, a donor database or a fundraising mailing system for another.

But important as they are, the introduction of these company-specific, tactical systems and processes will not in itself move the organization out of Whitewater and into Predictable Success. For that to happen, a more fundamental, foundational set of systems and processes is required—systems and processes that are not just specific to any one business, but needed by *every* organization in order to emerge from Whitewater.

## Overcoming Complexity

Think for a moment about the underlying issue faced by the organization in Whitewater: *dealing with complexity*.

Back when the business was in Fun, everything was relatively simple: a smaller number of employees, a direct line of sight from management to the front line, a simpler product line, fewer customers and suppliers—less "moving parts" in general. Then the business grows: more people, more products, less transparency, more complexity . . . and eventually, as we've seen, the organization slides into Whitewater.

To identify those systems and processes needed to get the organization *out* of Whitewater, we need to answer this question: When it arrives, what does complexity actually change? Put another way, in its day-to-day operations, how does the management of a complex organization vary, compared to that of a simpler organization?

The answer will be painfully familiar to anyone involved with managing a complex entity: *decision making*. Making and executing decisions is much harder in a complex organization than it is in a simple one. In Fun, decisions are made frequently and almost instantly, often based on instinct. Implementation of those decisions is quick and transparent; the outcome is usually obvious; and if a decision doesn't produce the required result, iterative changes can be made swiftly until the desired outcome is achieved. As a result, the Fun organization is flexible, light on its feet and responsive to customer needs.

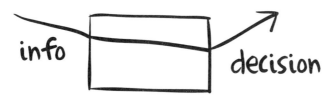

Figure 9.1 Decision Making in Fun

Contrast that with the decision-making process once the organization hits the complexity of Whitewater: The sheer number of decisions to be made (and the amount of data supporting them) has increased perpendicularly; the number of people involved in the decision-making process has multiplied; who should be involved in any specific decision is not always clear; and the individuals responsible for implementing most decisions are two or three steps removed from those making the decisions in the first place.

As a result, in Whitewater the time involved—in first recognizing the need to make a decision, then making the decision, implementing it, and receiving feedback as to whether or not it has worked—grows exponentially. It becomes more and more difficult for the organization to make and implement effective decisions, until eventually the decision-making process slows to a crawl, and in the worst cases may grind to a halt.

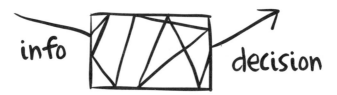

Figure 9.2 Decision Making in Whitewater

In the more extreme cases of Whitewater, perfectly good decisions languish unimplemented, or are launched with initial high hopes only to whither and fade in a short time. The organization becomes confused, frozen in inaction and unresponsive to the needs of customers—all despite the desire of increasingly frustrated management to be quite the opposite.

## Building a Machine for Decision Making

So, to get out of Whitewater and into Predictable Success, the key systems and processes that management must implement are those that will provide a new structure for *making and implementing decisions*—a decision-making structure that is capable of mastering the new complexities of the organization.

This calls first for management to acknowledge that the freewheeling, intuitive decision-making process of Fun cannot produce consistently effective results for the larger, more complex organization now in Whitewater. Management's challenge is to build a new, systematic process for making decisions—not a process that is staid, rigid and bureaucratic, but one that embraces the vision, enthusiasm, creativity, risk taking and entrepreneurial zeal that have propelled the organization's growth.

To build this new decision-making structure and process, management must achieve no less than a top-to-bottom reshaping of the organization, turning it from a personalized outward expression of the founder/owners—an organization greatly dependent on the founder/

owners' intuition, expertise, wisdom and knowledge—into a highly effective organism in its own right that can operate independently of the founder/owners: an organization that is in itself a machine for decision making.

To achieve this, there are six primary areas into which systems and processes must be introduced to change how the organization makes decisions:

# 1. The Organization Chart

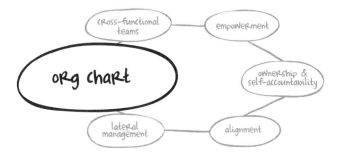

The organization chart in Whitewater (if the business has an organization chart at all) usually combines an aspirational representation of key functional roles with a declaration of seniority, but gives little indication of how the business is really controlled.

In other words, the key players will all be on the chart, they will likely all have titles and it will be clear who is senior to whom, but the lines on the organization chart will not reflect the day-to-day reality of how the business is actually *run*.

In Whitewater, real communications flow in different directions than the reporting lines indicate, and actual decisions are made outside the boxes on the org chart. Most real decisions are made by a small central group of key advisors to the founder/owners and are communicated unilaterally to those impacted. The members of this inner circle may appear anywhere—or not at all—on the org chart.

In Whitewater, a job title may or may not bring with it the authority to actually execute the responsibilities that come with it. Management meetings may or may not take place as scheduled, depending on the mood and other commitments of the founder/owner, and decisions made in any such meetings are entirely provisional, pending discussion by the inner circle.

To get out of Whitewater and into Predictable Success, management (fully supported and aided by the founder/owners) must recognize the lack of congruence between theory and reality, and begin by implementing three mundane, but essential changes:

**1.1 Redesign the organization chart to reflect operational reality.** This is a crucial first step in attaining genuine, lasting Predictable Success. The organization chart must reflect not relative power or status, nor a theorized, "textbook" representation of an idealized hierarchy, but the actual, real-world structure that is needed to manage the organization.

This calls for hard questions and honest debate. If there are (for example) three sales managers all currently on the organization chart at the same level of seniority, is one of them, in reality, the VP of Sales? If so, the organization chart should reflect that—even if the issue has been avoided up to now because of the possibility of offending the other two sales managers. If not, and all three sales managers are genuinely at the same level of responsibility, does that indicate that the business *needs* a VP of Sales? If that is the case, get the position on the chart and work out how it is going to be filled.

Is the founder/owner described on the existing org chart as the CEO, and if so, does she actually fulfill that role? Or in reality is she acting more as the company president or COO? If so, what are the implications of this? Do we need a CEO? Or should a COO take that role over from the founder/owner and allow her to act more as the CEO?

This questioning process needs to be applied all the way down the org chart: Is the "warehouse manager" on the org chart in fact acting as the VP of Operations? Or (more important) is the "VP of Operations" really acting as a warehouse manager? If so, and in all cases, the org chart should be redesigned to reflect the realities of (a) what the organization really needs in order to operate in Predictable Success, and (b) the actual roles the current incumbents are playing—not what their job titles say.

In all this, there is one touchstone concept that will guide the process greatly: *Separate the positions from the people, and concentrate on the positions.* When the business is growing up through Fun, key positions are highly identified with the people who inhabit them. In fact, in Fun, many positions in the business are really just an outgrowth of the *person*—Joe is the sales manager, and so the role of sales manager is whatever Joe does; Freda becomes the IT person because she happens to know about computers and everybody goes to her when they have an IT problem, and so the role of IT manager becomes whatever Freda does.

Moving into Predictable Success begins by recognizing that in order to achieve sustained success, the organization needs certain key positions to be filled—and filled effectively. It is the effective execution of those *positions* that is primary to the organization's long-term success, not dependence on whomever the current incumbent is. This is not to say that Joe and Freda are not excellent at their jobs (maybe they are, maybe they aren't), but rather that the organization must recognize the permanent, structural need for a sales manager and an IT manager, not a dependence on Joe or Freda.

**1.2 Define key management responsibilities clearly.** Once all the key positions needed by the organization have been clearly identified, the next step is to precisely define what is required from each of those positions—the duties and responsibilities of each key role.

Here again, it is essential to separate the *position* from the *person*. The question is not what is expected from (for example) Joe or Freda, but what is expected from a sales manager and an IT manager—specifically, what the rest of the organization expects and needs from those positions, independent of who might occupy the positions at any time.

The most effective way to do this is not by grabbing an off-the-shelf template or sample job description, but by involving the actual people who are most dependent on the effective functioning of the position—the position's internal and external customers, if you will.

The sales manager job description, for example, is in effect a contract between the sales manager and that role's manager, any direct reports, the admin department to whom the sales manager sends reports and order information, the ops staff who have to fulfill the sales, and the external customer to whom the sales are made. The best way to write such a job description? Pull together a representative team of each of the key internal and external customers listed above, and have them draft it out. After all, they are the people who are in the best position to know what is required of the sales manager position.

For the IT manager position, the team that can best write a real-world job specification might comprise that role's manager, direct reports (if any), one or two of the heavier IT users in the organization, and perhaps the accountant who sets the IT spending budget. These are the people representing the positions that the function exists to serve—so for the job description to be of genuine value, they should be involved in designing it.

This group of internal and external customers, facilitated by someone with no major stake in the outcome (to ensure that only reasonable expectations are included in the resulting job description), should be given the responsibility of setting the duties and responsibilities of each key position, together with quantitative metrics wherever possible. For example, the sales manager position might include metrics not only for the sales budgets but also for the percentage of incorrect or incomplete invoice details (from the admin department), the number of ride-alongs or customer visits made with direct reports, and the frequency of follow-up visits to top customers. Similarly, the IT manager position may include defined response times in the case of emergencies, the amount and timing of training provided to new employees, and the capital budget, all negotiated with the internal and external customers.

This method of redesigning job specifications can cause some conflict. An individual who has filled a particular role for some time (like Joe or Freda) may not see it as his or her job to do certain things proposed or requested by the group—and because the position has for so long been an outgrowth of the individual, rather than a defined position in its own right, there can be some historical justification for this stance. Also, the current incumbent may fear that the position is being redefined in ways that exceed his or her skill set and thus will cause them to fail or look bad.

These are hard issues, but they cannot be avoided—they are part of the growing pains every business experiences when moving from Whitewater into Predictable Success. Some organizations stumble at this stage, with management fearful of upsetting or losing key employees, and choosing to fudge the redefinition of job responsibilities or avoiding it altogether.

If you are tempted to skip this step, don't. It is important to understand this point: If you fail to redesign your key management roles for Predictable Success, you will not get there. Fudging or avoidance will result in the rest of the steps outlined in this chapter failing to take hold, because there isn't a strong enough organization chart to support them.

Instead, take time with each key employee to explain the distinction you are making between the position and the person. Make it clear that for the good of the organization as a whole it is imperative that there be a clear understanding of what is required from the *position*, separate from them as individuals. Assure them that you are not expecting that their skill set will transform overnight to meet the new requirements of the position, and that you will support them, with time and resources, in developing any new skills required by the redefined job specification. Work out a development program with them if appropriate, and find them a mentor if that would be helpful. Track their progress, and motivate and encourage them to grow into the newly defined roles.

Even with this approach, there will be times when you will conclude that the current incumbent is simply not capable of effectively filling the newly redefined position. When this happens, in all probability it will not be a surprise to you—you will likely have been harboring doubts about the individual's "fit" for the position in any case. Again, fudging or ignoring the situation will simply hinder, and possibly derail, your progress into Predictable Success. Leaving an ineffective, incompetent or underperforming person in a key position produces a fatal Achilles' heel: It will drain credibility, demotivate others and produce a bottleneck when you try to implement the other steps in this chapter. As before, it is better to face the situation, reposition the individual elsewhere in the organization or let him or her go, and begin anew the process of filling the position. In any case, you'll have to do it sometime—so why not do it now?

**1.3 Institute appropriate management teams and meetings.** Once the org chart and key job descriptions have been redesigned, the final phase in this step is to decide who needs to meet with whom in order to get effective decisions made.

Do you need a regular "all hands" management meeting? How often is regular? Who will chair it, and what will be discussed? If the CEO chairs it, what happens when he or she is not around? (Remember, we're trying to build a "machine" for decision-making—not something that is dependent on any one individual.)

What about elsewhere in the organization, apart from top management—who else needs to meet, and when? And what for? Don't forget, we want only those systems and processes (and that includes meetings) that are necessary—otherwise we risk pushing the organization too far and into Treadmill. How do we know what's needed and what isn't?

Thankfully, we've already done the hard work that will provide most of the answers we need: the other people who need to meet are the same people who redesigned the job specifications in section 1.2 above.

It's only logical that if, as a result of redesigning his job description, the sales manager has agreed "terms of engagement" with the chief purchasing clerk, his direct reports, his manager, and other internal and external customers, he should meet with them regularly to review progress. Similarly, the IT manager now also knows that to exchange the information necessary to do her job right, she needs to meet regularly with her manager, her direct reports, the one or two heavier IT users in the organization, and the accountant who sets the IT spending budget.

The frequency, length and content of those meetings will vary depending on the priority and importance of the underlying metric. Joe is likely to meet with his external customers more often than with the chief purchasing clerk, and Freda will meet with the accountant about her budget less frequently than she will meet with her internal "customers"—but the basic structure of who needs to meet with whom is clear from the redesigned job specifications. (We'll see how to structure other meetings, outside of those prompted by the redesigned job descriptions, in section 4 on cross-functional teams.)

Remember, meetings have no validity on their own—they're just a conduit for decision making. It's management's job to get the balance just right: Too few meetings in a complex organization and the decision-making process will fail; too many meetings and the organization is headed for Treadmill.

It is important to experiment with meetings to get their size and shape just right for delivering only what the organization needs—no more and no less. Try out different meeting styles (standing up, sitting down; in person or by phone; agenda or no agenda), different facilitators, different routines. Ask participants what works and what doesn't, and be prepared to change. Above all, if a meeting becomes a dry, rote recitation of information that few people are interested in, shut it down and start something fresh.

# 2. Lateral Management Roles

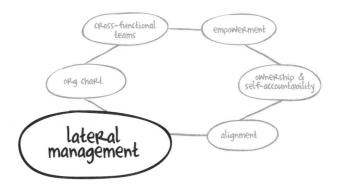

To move an organization from Whitewater to Predictable Success, the second area requiring management intervention is in how managers interact with each other.

Historically, managers appointed during Fun have a primarily vertical responsibility—*downward* to their direct reports, and *upward* to their boss (usually, though not always, the founder/owner). Also, because the organization isn't large enough yet to support or warrant a high level of bureaucracy, the managers generally continue to have substantial operational responsibilities in addition to their management duties: A sales manager will continue to also be a salesperson, a warehouse manager will continue to work on the warehouse floor, etc. Their managerial responsibilities are viewed as an "add-on" to the work they do from day to day, and their main—if not only—responsibilities as a manager are to corral, motivate and manage their direct reports and to report on progress or problems to their boss.

As a result, a manager appointed during Fun can continue to work happily in his or her own functional silo. For decision-making purposes, only limited contact with fellow managers is necessary.

Figure 9.3 Vertical Management Role in Fun

However, when the organization hits the complexity of Whitewater, managers increasingly need to interact with each other in order to get decisions made. Managers from sales, operations and administration find themselves entangled in a web of codependence that, because of the silos created during the Fun experience, they find frustrating.

For many managers, their mental image of management is based on the Fun experience—their role is to manage their boss and their functional team, vertically. All this other stuff—having to wrangle with a fellow manager to get paperwork cleared, lobby another manager to get the resources they need or argue with a third about the priority of a customer's needs, say—appears like so much flak and distraction, keeping them from their main jobs: managing their own team and getting on with meeting their day-to-day goals.

For the organization to successfully move into Predictable Success, senior management must recognize and enforce a new precept: that managers now have a dual role—to manage both *vertically* (down to their direct reports and up to their boss) and *laterally*, to their fellow managers.

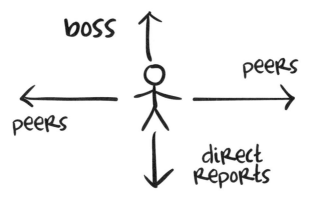

Figure 9.4 Vertical and Lateral Management Roles in Predictable Success

Moving managers from a solely vertical to a vertical-and-lateral mindset isn't always easy. Some managers will resent the imposition of what they see as unnecessary additional responsibilities. Others will embrace the idea but, lacking the management skills necessary to interact effectively with their colleagues, fail to implement it. In the worst cases, a manager may be exposed as having few or no interpersonal skills and will not only staunchly resist, but may actively fight against pressure to work collegially with peers.

Making the transition from vertical to vertical-and-lateral management roles requires determination, hard work and perseverance on the part of senior management. Managers are likely, whether consciously or subconsciously, to try to return to what seems to them the simpler, easier days of Fun management—just them and their team, enjoying limited contact with others outside their silo.

Achieving the switch from a vertical-only to a vertical-and-lateral management style is like a right-handed person learning how to write with the left hand—it requires a supremely conscious effort, and can feel tortuous at times. Here are some ways in which the transition can be accelerated:

**2.1 Make the addition of lateral management explicit.** Unless overtly told otherwise, most managers will mentally retain the Fun-based, vertical-only management model as the status quo. They will, at a subconscious level, be waiting for all these "issues" with other managers to be resolved, so they can go back to how things were—managing their own team vertically.

Senior management must take time to explain to every manager that those days are gone—that being a manager now permanently includes both vertical and lateral management roles.

**2.2 Have managers meet proactively, in a non-issue-based context.** We've already established that when Whitewater takes hold in an organization, managers are forced to interact with each other in order to resolve operational issues: Why is this paperwork you send me never completed correctly? Why are you ordering so many of the wrong materials? Why are deliveries to my customers so often late?

This focus on what are usually negative issues, while natural at the time, causes managers to view lateral interaction with their comanagers as being reactive, issue-based and confrontational. Blame and accusation become one side of peer interaction, with defensiveness and protectionism on the other. As a result, many managers want to avoid interaction if at all possible, and others wish to engage in it for the wrong reasons.

It is important for senior management to show that lateral management (interaction between peer managers) can and should be proactive, not reactive—problem-avoiding, rather than problem-solving (when possible)—collaborative, not confrontational.

To make this shift to proactive, problem-avoiding, collaborative lateral management, it is important to encourage managers to meet *ahead* of issues, rather than *about* issues—for the sales and operations managers to meet, for example, at the start of the month to plan customer delivery schedules, rather than at the end of the month to hold a post-mortem on why deliveries were too often late.

We've already seen in a previous point (1.3) that managers will be meeting regularly as part of the revised organization structure. It's important that those meetings are forward-looking and collaborative, not backward-looking and confrontational.

**2.3 Model the benefits of lateral management.** There is no better place to demonstrate the benefits of positive, proactive lateral management than at the very top of the organization. The organization's most senior executive—the founder/owner, CEO or president—can become an excellent role model by proactively consulting and collaborating with the senior management team.

This can be hard at first, particularly for those founder/owners who have been used to wielding absolute or near-absolute authority in the past. But by persevering and personally demonstrating the power of positive lateral management—for example, by including one or two senior managers in decisions on topics that they might once have reserved entirely to themselves (such as compensation)—senior executives can begin a cascading effect down through the senior management team to middle managers and team leaders.

**2.4 Hire new managers who can mentor others in lateral management.** One of the hurdles in getting from Whitewater to Predictable Success is that there may be few in the organization who have faced such a challenge before—and therefore few who understand how to address it.

This area—managing laterally as well as vertically—can be one such issue. Sometimes there are only one or two managers in the organization who have interacted in such a way before (occasionally, with a small team of founder/owners and a few loyal, Fun-appointed managers, there is no one).

Bear this in mind when hiring new managers, and seek to hire those who have worked successfully in a lateral management mode, and who can be a role model and mentor to others.

# 3. Alignment

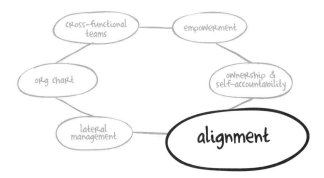

When growth tops out in late Fun and an organization begins to slide into Whitewater, one of the first indications that there are problems ahead is an increasing deterioration in cohesion and alignment throughout the organization.

In the early and middle stages of Fun, everyone in the organization is more or less on the same page, pointed in the same direction, trying to achieve the same goals for the organization as a whole. But as Whitewater takes hold, managers and their teams break into silos—they hunker down in their own operational "bunkers," waiting for the shaking of Whitewater to pass by, increasingly pursuing their own departmental or team agendas and acting independently of the rest of the organization.

Added to this, and partially because of it, a sense of drift emerges at the top of the organization. Senior management, whether it be the founder/owners or a management team, loses its previously unerring sense of purpose, and for a while there is a sense of inaction, a lack of direction throughout the organization.

Management then attempts to correct this, reaching out for solutions to the frustrating inertia. "Ditch to ditch" management arrives as initiatives and methodologies replace one another as the fad of the month. (It is this pattern—stagnant lull followed by the introduction of successively fervid initiatives and programs—that produces the Whitewater feeling of the business being violently rocked from side to side.)

Taken together, these symptoms of Whitewater (a directionless vacuum, then repeated attempts to fill the vacuum with programs and initiatives) dissipate the previously high degree of alignment in the organization. Depending on the leadership of their direct manager, employees either lose their personal vision of where the organization is going (and how they can contribute to that journey) or develop a vision limited to their own silo, different from and possibly competing with that of other silos in the organization.

Either way, the net effect is that instead of pulling together in one direction, individual employees in the organization each end up pulling in different directions—a corporate version of Brownian motion that makes the organization dysfunctional at best, and nearly paralyzed at worst.

Management's third key task in getting out of Whitewater and into Predictable Success is to restore alignment to the entire organization, by ensuring (as much as possible) that everyone is once more pulling in the same direction.

The three steps to achieving this are as follows:

**3.1 Do it at the right time.** Restoring a sense of alignment can be achieved only *after* the organization chart has been redesigned and lateral management has been introduced (see sections 1 and 2 above).

This is because only when managers know their sense of place in the organization chart, understand clearly their duties and responsibilities, and most important, have learned to work with each other as peers will they be able to see the importance of working together on the common goal of organization-wide alignment and have the working relationships to achieve it.

**3.2 Revisit the organization's mission, vision and values.** During the period of fast, early growth in Fun, most organizations have a clear sense of their own identity. Most people working for young, vibrant organizations know what it is that defines the organization, that makes it what it is and sets it apart from its competitors.

Organizations that have taken longer to get to Whitewater (or have slipped back into it from Predictable Success) often have this sense of identity formally incorporated into a mission statement, a vision statement, a values statement or some version of all three.

When the organization slides into Whitewater, that sense of identity shrinks as the alignment between employees dissipates. This is unfortunate, but logical—after all, in an organization, what else is a sense of identity other than a shared sense of who we are? Once the alignment between employees goes, our shared sense of identity goes too.

In Whitewater, it isn't long before the company's carefully crafted mission statement begins to seem irrelevant, or worse, hollow. Previously beloved and believed mantras ("Total quality!" or "100% customer satisfaction!" or "We walk the extra mile so you don't have to!") become embarrassments, and the banners on the warehouse wall proclaiming them seem almost like taunts.

To correct this, just as the organization's identity withered because employee alignment dissipated, now management must reverse the process and reintroduce a strong sense of identity around which employee alignment can rebuild.

In practical terms, this means reassessing the organization's mission, vision, and values in the light of recent history and its new operating realities and aspirations—in other words, taking a long, hard look at who you really are as an organization trying to make it to Predictable Success—not what you were in the glory days of Fun.

To do this effectively, count on spending one or two days with the management team and whoever else you feel can contribute positively. (Hint: Your customers and line employees have a lot of useful stuff to say about "who you are" as an organization, and sometime senior managers are the ones who are most locked into the past.)

Sometimes such a reassessment will result in a whole new identity—new mission, new vision, new values. Sometimes the old identity will re-emerge, still intact but revitalized. Most often the result is somewhere in between: a combination of old and new. Either way, the most important thing is that you  guide the organization through a rediscovery of its true identity—an identity around which everyone, with integrity, can once more align.

**3.3 Break up clique- and silo-based alignment.** After the revitalization of the company's mission, vision and values, the last symptom of organizational alignment for management to address is that of "silos"—cliques, usually (but not always) in functional groups typically led by their line manager, that have developed different visions of "who we are."

Silos are not a bad thing in and of themselves—their existence is an unavoidable reality in any relatively complex organization—but in Whitewater (and in Treadmill, as we'll see in a later chapter) they present a peculiar barrier to getting to Predictable Success. As we've already seen, when an organization is in Whitewater, silos slow the organization's progress to Predictable Success by diluting alignment.

This happens as a direct result of the loss of direction by senior management that we've discussed above—when senior management loses direction, the more strong-minded line managers (it could be anyone, but it's usually the line manager) step in to fill the void and, in order to keep their employees motivated, substitute the "lost" sense of direction, vision and values with their own.

This can happen either benevolently, with the manager simply trying to fill a dangerous vacuum, or as a power grab, with the manager using the vacuum as an opportunity to extend his or her influence. Either way, it doesn't really matter—the important thing is that the net effect is to further wrench the organization out of alignment by developing cliques with competing—or at least nonaligned—vision and values.

In my experience, around 70 percent to 80 percent of the work involved in breaking up clique- and silo-based alignment and replacing it with organization-wide alignment is achieved simply by implementing the step above—a rejuvenation and reintroduction of the company's mission, vision and values. Most employees respond intuitively, and by preference, to an organization-wide vision rather than a department-only vision.

But what of the remaining 20 percent to 30 percent of managers who continue to dance to their own tune—leading their followers with a banner of their own rather than rallying to the company flag?

Such managers, if they don't willingly respond to coaching from senior management, are essentially indicating that they don't share management's vision of taking the organization to Predictable Success. Instead they see their role as rooted in the managerially autonomous days of Fun, when the role of the manager was solely to manage vertically, and when he or she was free to "brand" the team with its own identity, so long as it achieved the primary functional goals.

In essence, this is another symptom of a manager who will not accept a lateral management role and who, if the organization is to get to Predictable Success, must be replaced. This is often a hard thing for management to

> Section 3.3 might sound somewhat totalitarian, and give the impression that to be in Predictable Success there must be no dissent or difference of opinion within the organization. In fact (as we'll see), nothing could be further from the truth—it's simply that at this stage in the organization's development, it is crucial for everyone in the organization to regroup around a common set of shared goals in order to push forward into Predictable Success. Once there, variety and diversity can (and will) flourish once more.

accept—especially if the manager has been with the organization for some time, and even more so if he or she is one of the Big Dogs that helped build the business to where it is now. But it is one of the "growing pains" on the path from Whitewater to Predictable Success, a decision that, if avoided, will halt the organization's transition to Predictable Success.

# 4. Cross-functional Teams

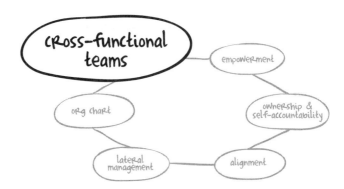

The fourth aspect of decision making faced by an organization trying to get from Whitewater to Predictable Success is getting its workforce to engage cross-functionally—not just occasionally, but consistently and by default.

We've already seen that in order to *make* decisions, the managers in the organization need to relate laterally with each other, in addition to managing "vertically" to their direct reports and bosses. When it comes to *implementing* those decisions, the same principle applies to the workforce in general: In order to successfully implement, they need to learn (or more likely, relearn) how to work across functions, and not just in their own silos.

The reason for this will by now be obvious: managing the increasing complexity that propelled the organization into Whitewater requires the deployment of expertise, knowledge and experience from all parts of the organization. Few decisions—and none that are of significance—are capable of being made or implemented within the tight confines of just one functional area.

The good news is that by and large, this is not a question of teaching the workforce new skills. Many of the employees will have automatically worked cross-functionally during the early and middle stages of Fun (they just wouldn't have used the phrase "cross-functional"). In Fun, it's natural to walk down the corridor to see whomever needs to be seen in order to get something done. It's only in the late stages of Fun and in Whitewater that the force of complexity begins to produce silos and eradicate cross-functionality.

So, enabling employees to return to working cross-functionally consistently and by default usually isn't difficult, as long as four principles are applied:

**4.1 Do it in the right sequence.** As with the issue of alignment, it's foolish to try to get employees working cross-functionally if their managers aren't modeling the same thing. Don't try to move on this area until your managers are consistently and successfully relating laterally. If you try to encourage cross-functionality too early, it will lack credibility among the line employees (who will look to the managers and see no such thing happening) and may well be undermined by the managers themselves, who will not yet have seen the benefits of working in this manner.

**4.2 Tell it like it is—often.** As we've seen in so many cases, getting to Predictable Success requires senior management to make clear its expectations and to reinforce them consistently. Leaving expectations unsaid, easing off on those expectations, or letting things slide is the equivalent of going down a chute in Chutes and Ladders—it causes the organization to go backward in its development.

The rule applies just as much to working cross-functionally: Management must explain clearly what it requires of its employees (in this case, to work cross-functionally, consistently and by default), reinforce that message regularly, reward compliance and punish deliberate defiance.

Turning a blind eye or letting things slide when faced with recalcitrance is not an option; allowing a Big Dog to flaunt management's expectations on cross-functionality and continue to work outside the system as a "maverick" will delay, and in extreme cases prevent, the organization's transition to Predictable Success. Less acceptable still (as we saw in point 3.3) is when a manager persists in encouraging his or her entire team to work in a silo, without cross-functional interaction.

**4.3 Use cross-functional teams as training wheels.** The ultimate goal is to get each individual employee to the point where, when faced by a decision, he or she instinctively thinks and acts cross-functionally, so that rather like the body's brain, neuron system and limbs, the whole organization reacts and responds naturally and seamlessly to the business's moment-by-moment needs and intentions.

To get there will almost certainly require the use of some "training wheels" at the outset—artificial structures that act as reminders to think, act and decide cross-functionally, and that will prevent employees from hunkering down in their silos.

The simplest version of this is the cross-functional team—a formally constituted group of employees from throughout the organization, tasked with making or implementing a specific decision or group of decisions.

Examples might be the design of a new product delivery process, a new employee orientation program or rethinking the company's website.

Setting up one or two cross-functional teams is a great way to jumpstart the process of getting everyone to think and act cross-functionally—but don't overdo it: One or two cross-functional teams are more than enough to begin with. Any more than that will drain too much of your employees' time and energy, and will slow down, rather than accelerate, the organization's transition into Predictable Success.

**4.4 Start with hiring.** A great place to begin with cross-functional teams is in the hiring process. We've already seen the importance of involving people from throughout the organization in order to make successful hires, and most employees can see the benefits immediately. Discussing the competing merits of potential employees and making the final hiring decision is a great way to build cross-functional "muscle" in the organization.

# 5. Empowerment

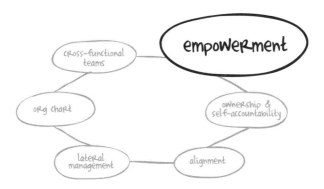

Once managers have been effective in relating laterally with each other for a while, and after a few cross-functional teams have worked together successfully, both groups—managers and employees alike—begin not just to trust, but increasingly to depend on the cross-functional process to produce effective decisions and successfully implement them.

This increasing trust in cross-functional decision making—together with a functioning organization chart, clarified job descriptions, lateral management roles and realigned employees—enables the organization to begin the process of regaining control over its own destiny.

As the decision-making process unfreezes and more high-quality decisions are made and acted upon, management realizes that now, at last, when it puts its foot on the pedal, the organization moves forward (albeit slowly, at present). The business has begun the transition into Predictable Success.

A common mistake at this stage is to try to accelerate the process and complete the transition by creating even more cross-functional teams—a natural response, as it appears obvious that the introduction of cross-functional teams was what finally pushed the organization forward.

As we've already seen, adding more cross-functional teams too early has the opposite effect: It slows down the organization's developmental growth by draining too much of employees' time and energy. Too many cross-functional teams become a drag on the organization (too many meetings, not enough time), and eventually participants burn out, the practice loses its attraction and finally, the whole cross-functional process collapses under its own weight, sending the organization right back to the start of Whitewater.

Much more effective in accelerating the organization's move into Predictable Success is to *intensify* rather than *dilute* the outputs from the existing cross-functional activities—specifically, this means adding more empowerment to the cross-functional process by providing the small number of cross-functional teams with more authority and broader responsibilities than before.

Think of this as going deeper with cross-functionality rather than spreading it wider.

There are a three reasons why this works so well in accelerating the transition to Predictable Success:

**5.1 Success builds success.** Successful lateral engagement by managers and productive cross-functionality by employees together create a desire on everyone's part to "go deeper"—to see if even more can be achieved from the process. After a few months of demonstrable success, managers become less wary of what the cross-functional teams are doing, and are more prepared to delegate some of their authority to them. For their part, the employees are more confident in their own ability to make and implement good decisions, and are eager to reach higher.

**5.2 Empowerment scales the cross-functional process in a sustainable way.** Empowering existing cross-functional teams with more authority and responsibility accelerates the personal skills development of the individuals on those teams, by requiring more from them, setting higher challenges and stretching their decision-making faculties.

This provides managers with a trusted cohort of seasoned individuals with whom they can later "seed" additional cross-functional activities, and who can in turn mentor and coach others. This way, cross-functional decision making can spread through the organization without burning out participants ill-equipped to participate.

Secondly, by using a multiplier effect (the initial cadre of individuals experienced in cross-functional decision-making coach others to develop similar skills, who in turn coach others, who in turn coach others), over time the organization's dependence on the use of cross-functional teams as training wheels is lessened, as more and more individuals learn and relearn to think, act, and make cross-functional decisions naturally and by default.

**5.3 Empowerment breeds expectancy.** Witnessing a small number of cross-functional groups succeed, and then being empowered to do even more, builds desire on the part of others to get in on the action—much more so than if management were to simply add more cross-functional teams and co-opt others to join the process.

Multiplying and mandating the use of too many cross-functional teams too early in the transition to Predictable Success leads to a perception of these terms as sterile and mechanical time wasters. Conversely, achieving early successes with just one or two teams, then amplifying the success of those teams, enhances the perception of cross-functional decision making as a vital and powerful tool.

By, in a sense, limiting supply, the attraction of cross-functional teams is increased, and the enthusiastic participation of others later on is more likely.

# 6. Ownership and Self-accountability

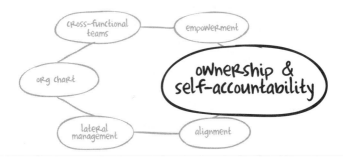

The sixth and final step in moving from Whitewater to Predictable Success is the reignition of a sense of ownership and self-accountability throughout the entire organization.

Of everything discussed in this chapter, the concept of ownership and self-accountability is the single most important factor contributing to Predictable Success. As we'll see in the next two chapters, not only does the reemergence of ownership and self-accountability push the organization over the edge into Predictable Success, but its continued existence is the lynchpin that keeps the organization in Predictable Success, preventing it from sliding back into Whitewater or forward into Treadmill.

So, what does "ownership and self-accountability" mean?

In the context of Predictable Success, it denotes an innate belief on the part of the employees that they "own" all aspects of their job, and that aside from any formal accountability they may be subject to, the employee hold *themselves* accountable for their performance and for the successful completion of tasks delegated to them.

Typically, the sense of ownership and self-accountability is at its highest in Fun. The close involvement of the founder/owners in hiring decisions means that employees are generally hired only if they have a strong sense of ownership and self-accountability to begin with, and in any case, the extreme transparency in the organization means that there is nowhere for an unengaged employee to hide.

When Whitewater strikes, the loss of vision and alignment on the part of employees, the increasing separation of the hiring process from the founder/owners, and the lack of transparency caused by complexity together cause ownership and self-accountability to wither. These are replaced with a sense of powerlessness ("It doesn't matter what I do, because nobody notices or cares"), and in extreme cases apathy ("Nobody knows what they're doing around here, so why should I knock myself out?").

One of the biggest management challenges in Whitewater is that the disappearance of ownership and self-accountability turns management into a "push" process, where managers have to personally oversee and push through the implementation of every important management decision, because their employees aren't taking the ball and running with it themselves. When it finally arrives, the widespread reemergence of ownership and self-accountability reorients management to a "pull" process—where instead of whip-wielding overseers, managers become a resource to their team members, who themselves take ownership of implementation.

This return of ownership and self-accountability and the resulting shift from "push" to "pull" management constitute the final dynamic change that completes the transition of the organization from Whitewater into Predictable Success.

There are four key factors that dictate the reemergence of ownership and self-accountability in the organization:

**6.1 It cannot be forced or mandated.** If ownership and self-accountability comprise the key dynamic that pushes the organization from Whitewater into Predictable Success, then why not simply instill it into the organization much earlier, when the organization first slips into Whitewater?

Answer: Because it can't be done. A large part of the Amazonian rain forest has been given over to books and articles striving to show how to enforce ownership and self-accountability in organizations. But the truth is that ownership and self-accountability cannot be mandated—it is an inner commitment made voluntarily by an individual and can only be encouraged, at best. Trying to force ownership and self-accountability on employees who have no internal motivation to be so is fruitless.

In an example of supreme irony, this is not only the one factor among the six discussed in this chapter that is the most powerful, it is also the one that is least under the direct control of management.

**6.2 It will only emerge if and when the other five steps are successfully implemented.** So if management has no direct control over and cannot enforce ownership and self-accountability, does that mean that getting to Predictable Success is a matter of dumb luck and patience? Must management simply wait and hope that ownership and self-accountability will return?

Thankfully, not at all. In fact, by simply providing the right environment, like summer butterflies, ownership and self-accountability will return of their own volition. And guess what? The five steps we've already discussed in this chapter provide exactly the right environment for ownership and self-accountability to return to the organization and to flourish.

Employees who have been disoriented by the violent rocking of Whitewater will begin to recover their ownership and self-accountability only when they see the organization stabilize and lose its dysfunctionality. Specifically, they need to see managers working together in harmonious accord, and their colleagues once more working cross-functionally rather than in silos.

In other words, as management successfully and consistently implements the first five steps detailed in this chapter—a working organization chart, lateral management roles, alignment, cross-functionality and empowerment—so ownership and self-accountability will emerge spontaneously as employees reengage, excited by the reinvigoration of the organization and the renewed clarity of its vision.

**6.3 It will be resisted by some managers.** The transition of an organization from Whitewater to Predictable Success is, as we've already seen, a litmus test for some managers. Those managers who see their role as authority-based rather than leadership-based may resist emerging ownership and self-accountability in their direct reports because it appears (to them at least) to erode their own position by reducing their team members' reliance on them.

Depending on the manager's position in the organization and on his or her ability and inclination to be coached into a leadership-based management model, such managers may need to be replaced if the organization is to successfully complete its transition into Predictable Success.

**6.4 It will isolate poor hires.** As most of the workforce rediscovers its sense of ownership and self-accountability and enthusiastically recommits to the organization's renewed mission, vision and values, those employees who are "clock punchers"—only interested in doing the bare minimum to fulfill their responsibilities—will become increasingly isolated, as will those who have no real desire to work cross-functionally.

In making the final transition to Predictable Success, it is highly likely that management will need to weed out some employees who were able to slide by in the confusion and lack of transparency during Whitewater, but whose lack of ownership and self-accountability becomes increasingly apparent as the organization moves, finally, into Predictable Success.

## SUMMARY

- To move from Whitewater into Predictable Success, management needs to make six specific changes to the way in which the organization makes decisions.

- First, it must redesign its organization chart into a *machine for decision making*.

- Second, managers must learn to relate laterally—to each other—in addition to retaining their existing "vertical" relationships to their boss and their direct reports.

- Third, the newly aligned managers must push alignment down through the whole organization, renewing and invigorating their employees' understanding of and commitment to the organization's mission, vision and values.

- Fourth, management must implement and enforce cross-functional decision making throughout the organization.

- Fifth, the groups that are working cross-functionally must (over time) be empowered to assume more delegated authority and responsibility.

- Sixth, and finally, ownership and self-accountability will spontaneously reemerge in the workforce as a result of the first five steps, providing the final push into Predictable Success.

- There will be managers and employees opposed to each of the six steps, and management may need to consider if these individuals can remain with the organization if it is to get to Predictable Success.

# [ CHAPTER TEN ]

## WHAT TO DO WHEN YOU'VE OVERSHOT: RECOVERING FROM TREADMILL

"If we want, we can cloak ourselves in the myth of the professional manager and hide any
problem in a process flowchart."
—Jeffrey Immelt, CEO, GE

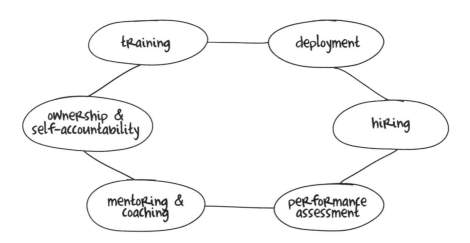

AS WE'VE SEEN THROUGHOUT THIS BOOK, THE MAIN DANGER FACING
an organization once it reaches Predictable Success is that management
may overcook its focus on systems and process, resulting in an overmanaged business that slides, silently and unnoticed, into Treadmill.

What makes the slide into Treadmill so hard to spot is that though ultimately destructive, it is both slow and (seemingly) natural.

*Natural* because a focus on systems and processes was the highly successful "Aha!" that pulled the business out of the spiraling chaos of Whitewater into Predictable Success—and continuing to introduce systems and processes in as many other parts of the organization as possible appears entirely reasonable to management.

*Slow* because rather like the human aging process, the slide into Treadmill happens in small, incremental steps—it isn't something that one notices every day. Managers typically don't see—let alone fret about—small, incremental losses in organizational versatility as a result of systematization. But those small, incremental losses accumulate over time until, after months or years, someone in senior management looks in the corporate mirror and sees an organization that has lost its edge, its flexibility and its lead over the competition.

For management, therefore, halting the slide into Treadmill, then reversing course back into Predictable Success, poses two challenges:

1. If the process is slow and incremental, how do we spot that it is happening in the first place?

2. If the problem is caused by an overdependence on systems and processes, what tools do we use to get back to Predictable Success? Put another way, how can systems and processes be introduced that in themselves *reduce* our dependence on systems and processes?

# It's the People, Stupid

The answer to both questions is one word: *people*. It is the people of the organization who will (if empowered to do so) reverse its decline into Treadmill. And it is here—on its people—that management must focus if it is to return the organization to Predictable Success.

Just as getting out of Whitewater required management to build systems and processes for *effective decision making*, so getting out of Treadmill will require management to build systems and processes around its *people*.

In doing so, rather like adding water to neat whiskey, management will restore the balance required for the organization to return to Predictable Success—the balance between systems and vision, process and creativity, and form and function that is lost in Treadmill.

To understand why adding yet more systems and processes around people restores the balance in the organization and returns it to Predictable Success (rather than driving it deeper into Treadmill, as one would expect), we need to look a little more closely under the hood at what actually happens when the organization is pushed into Treadmill in the first place.

As we've already seen, the introduction of systems and processes during Whitewater pushes the organization into Predictable Success. Then, as management becomes overreliant on those very systems and processes, the organization slides into Treadmill. But what is the underlying cause of the slide into Treadmill? What does overdependence on systems and processes actually *do* that begins the slide?

The reason the organization declines into Treadmill is not because of the overreliance on systems and processes per se; it is because of the resulting loss of knowledge, ability and flexibility on the part of the *users* of those systems and processes—the organization's employees. It is what the overreliance on systems and processes does to *people* that is the key factor in Treadmill, not the existence of systems and processes in and of themselves.

Just as a single guy with access to a fridge and a convenience store may forget (or never learn) how to cook, so the shop clerk using a point-of-sale machine that does every calculation for him forgets (or never learns) how to make change. The sales rep with a sales script and a checklist forgets (or never learns) how to genuinely relate to his customer. The manager with a quarterly rolling target, a monthly budget, a weekly action plan, a daily report sheet and an hourly time sheet forgets (or never learns) how to engage, inspire and motivate her team. The CEO with annual shareholder meetings, quarterly board meetings, monthly management meetings, weekly operations meetings, daily performance metrics and a schedule with the next open slot five weeks away forgets (or never learns) how to dream, innovate and create.

And so, once in Predictable Success, as the people in the organization slowly begin to depend more and more on systems and processes, so the creeping tendrils of those same systems and process slowly begin to choke the creativity, the innovation and the entrepreneurial, visionary, risk taking lifeblood out of the organization, and it begins its inexorable slide into Treadmill.

The answer is not in dismantling the existing systems and processes —that will simply drive the organization straight back to Whitewater. The answer is to change the way in which the employees *use* those systems and processes.

Just as the single guy living alone may—if so motivated—choose to visit the local market once a week and make one home-cooked meal, what if the shop clerk were prompted to periodically make the change calculation himself mentally, before checking with the till? What if the sales rep were encouraged to set aside his sales script once in a while, in order to genuinely and passionately engage with his potential customer first, with no agenda? What if the line manager were challenged to delegate the keeping of her hourly time sheet and daily action plan to her assistant, in order to spend the extra time mentoring one of her team members? What if the CEO discovered the value of setting every Thursday morning aside as a "come-all-ye" when she will meet, unscheduled, with any of her team who are in the vicinity—or if she were motivated to block out one week each year to simply go away and think strategically about the business?

In each hypothetical case, in ways large and small, these people are *using* systems and processes, rather than letting the systems and processes use *them*. In doing so, they become the organization's bulwark against sliding into Treadmill—or, if the organization is already in Treadmill, its most powerful tool in stopping that slide and returning to Predictable Success.

But management cannot simply hope that its people will see the need to do all of this, consistently and unprompted. Counter-intuitively, management needs to put in place *new* systems and processes—to motivate, prompt, inspire and equip its people to use existing systems and processes correctly.

Put simply, it is by *using systems and processes to change how your people use systems and process* that you will halt and reverse the slide into Treadmill, and make it back to Predictable Success.

These new, dynamic systems and processes that will counterbalance the more rigorous, mechanical systems and processes introduced in Whitewater are specifically required in six areas. Let's look at each in turn:

# 1. Hiring

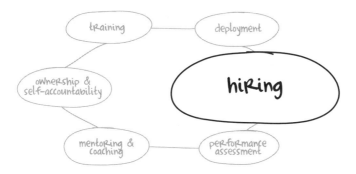

The first "people area" to focus on is the hiring process—the spring at the head of the river.

As in Chapter 9, the sequence here is important: There is little point in working with the other five people areas that follow if you haven't first ensured that the quality of people entering the organization is right to begin with.

Also, taking a detailed, formal look at your hiring process is the single step in this chapter that will most avoid a continued decline toward The Big Rut. Poor hiring in Treadmill (specifically, hiring people who are attracted to the oversystematized Treadmill culture) will amplify rather than reduce the organization's downward slide, pushing it further toward The Big Rut rather than back toward Predictable Success.

There are four steps an organization in Treadmill can take to refresh its hiring process so that it helps to arrest and reverse that decline, rather than amplify it:

**1.1 Don't "hire from within" or "hire externally"; hire competitively.** Organizations in Treadmill often emphasize a "we hire from within" policy. This happens for a number of reasons—a desire to maintain a sense of "family"; loyalty to existing employees; because it's easier to assess the candidate; because the learning curve is shorter; because it increases the likelihood that the candidate will "fit"; or because it's cheaper. For all these reasons, a "we hire from within" policy can seem both commendable and prudent.

In fact, overemphasis on internal hiring amplifies the downward momentum in Treadmill, toward The Big Rut, and does not help the organization get back to Predictable Success. This is so because internal hiring more often than not rewards the very practices that have started the decline into Treadmill in the first place: overdependence on systems and processes and slavish compliance to standards and practices.

The flawed logic works like this: Systems and processes are good, so compliance with systems and processes is good. We reward what is good, so we reward compliance to systems and processes. So the people who comply with systems and processes get promoted. Those who rock the boat do not. (Remember Whitewater—that was enough boat-rocking for quite a while, thank you.)

Unfortunately, a little constructive boat-rocking is exactly what the organization in Treadmill needs—and more compliance is exactly what it *doesn't* need. So a too-strong emphasis on internal hiring becomes an *amplifier* of Treadmill—by promoting the very people who are causing it—rather than a tool for escaping it.

The answer is not to shift to purely external hiring—that merely causes high turnover, strips the organization of the great experience and knowledge of the existing workforce, and dilutes the organization's cultural cohesion.

The right answer is to make every hire a competitive process—internal candidates are welcome to apply but will compete alongside high-quality external candidates. This forces a number of changes in the hiring dynamic: Internal candidates know they must actually have the skills required to perform in the new job, rather than simply depending on longevity and being there already to secure the position; hiring managers get to see and hear new ideas and new approaches to the job from the external candidates; and positions are filled with a mix of internal and external hires, with neither predominating.

Most important, the hiring process stops being a Treadmill amplifier that automatically promotes those who are part of the problem.

**1.2 Move people sideways.** For a larger organization, hiring competitively (point 1 above) will require looking creatively at how to fulfill the career aspirations of those employees who may now believe they are blocked from upward promotion.

Thinking creatively is in itself a good thing for an organization in Treadmill to be doing in any case, and here—in the hiring arena—it can be particularly beneficial. The answer lies in developing positive sideways career moves—encouraging employees to move *within* the organization to free up their career development options.

Making this option available—think of it as the equivalent of introducing the knight's move in chess—has the added benefit of moving people outside of their comfort zones, away from the systems and processes they have been immersed in, into new functional areas where they bring a new set of eyes and can use their institutional knowledge and experience to question how and why things are done in a certain way—exactly what the organization in Treadmill needs.

**1.3 Use a defined, cross-functional hiring process.** Letting a hiring manager appoint people to new positions entirely on his or her own is a recipe for Treadmill amplification. Left to our own devices, most of us will hire someone who reflects existing acceptable attitudes and approaches, and in Treadmill those attitudes and approaches are exactly what we need to shake up.

The pressure to conform in Treadmill is high, and so it is a rare manager who will go out of his or her way to hire someone who might be an irritant (even a constructive, positive irritant).

The answer is to use a well-defined, cross-functional hiring panel (including the hiring manager) and to give explicit instructions and guidance about the attitudes and attributes required in new hires (more about those in a moment). Despite the many managerial protestations that "I always try to hire people better/smarter than me," the evidence strongly points to the fact that this is far more likely to actually happen if the manager is part of a cross-functional hiring team that is following a well-defined hiring process and keeping everyone honest.

**1.4 Look for active curiosity alongside compliance skills.** Back when the organization began its move from Whitewater into Predictable Success, one of the changes we saw in the hiring process was that management would actively look to hire people who had experience in successfully working with systems and processes, to compensate for a lack of that experience within the organization.

Now, with the organization in Treadmill, the hiring imperative alters once more. While the need for compliance remains, it becomes important to add another desired trait: active curiosity. The organization does not need—indeed it must repudiate—*mindless* compliance. What is needed in Treadmill are people who, while quite capable of complying with the needs of complex systems and processes, also challenge those same systems and processes when necessary.

The hiring process should include behaviorally based questions, role play, case studies and testing to ensure that new employees bring the trait of active curiosity to the organization.

The first step on the path back to Predictable Success from Treadmill is to redesign your hiring process by making every post competitive, encouraging sideways moves in the organization, using a clearly defined cross-functional hiring panel and elevating curiosity as a hiring must-have.

# 2. Deployment

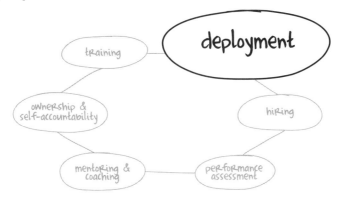

The second people area for the management of an organization in Tread-mill to review is how it deploys its employees once they are hired.

Truth be told, most organizations think very little about how their employees are deployed: Typically once they're hired, they're put through a little orientation, then shipped off to do the job they were hired for. Simple, right?

But think about how this casual process amplifies the decline of an organization in Treadmill: The employee, hired to do a job that is at present oversystematized and overprocessed, is put through an orientation program that explains exactly how to follow those same systems and processes, then is led to his or her work area to—guess what?—follow those selfsame systems and processes.

For the new employee of an organization in Treadmill, there is little or no opportunity to question why these systems and processes are being followed, or how they might be improved. The whole tenor of the deployment process is typically paternalistic, designed to assure the employee (and perhaps even the managers themselves) that everything is as it should be, and that systems and processes should be complied with without contention.

In order to stop the decline into Treadmill and reverse direction back to Predictable Success, management must address three specific aspects of the deployment of its employees:

**2.1 Emphasize "why" over "what," in a dialogue-based orientation that involves senior management.** Most orientation programs are (to use a word already introduced) paternalistic monologues. Corporate trainers or overworked managers talk about the history of the organization, what the new employee will do and how he or she will do it, then tack on a bit about the culture and mission of the organization. As we've seen, this approach merely solidifies the Treadmill organization's thrall to oversystematization.

To get out of Treadmill, it is important that the orientation process changes from a monologue about the "what" or "how" of the new employee's responsibilities and duties to a dialogue about the "why"—why the employee is doing things in the first place.

These two changes—encouraging employees to consider *why* they do what they do, and facilitating a dialogue about it—help to deconstruct the organization's systems and processes, bringing them out into the air and exposing them to analysis and critique.

If that analysis and critique is facilitated by senior managers rather than corporate trainers or line managers (who likely feel constrained to defend and support the status quo), so much the better. For an organization in Treadmill, putting open-minded, nondefensive senior managers in the bullpen with new employees and having an open and frank discussion about not just "what we do" but "why we do it" is one of the single most effective ways to reverse course back to Predictable Success.

**2.2 Use fixed-term postings.** In most organizations, a new employee is appointed to a post that remains his or her default position until and unless a new position opens up, or the employee decides to leave.

Such an approach fails to extract the best from employees at any time, but in Treadmill the effect is deadly. Keeping one person in one place for a long time intensifies the overdependence on a role-specific set of systems and processes. The employee "sentenced to life" in one position in the organization may enthusiastically show initiative early on and try to streamline and improve the systems and processes he or she works with, but over time inertia and the status quo almost always win out, and the employee settles into a dry routine that becomes hard-wired and inviolable.

To get out of Treadmill, employees should spend a maximum of three years or so in any one position before being rotated into a different job. This way, a new set of eyes is regularly brought to bear on each job and on its associated systems and processes.

**2.3 Promote the use of sabbaticals, shadowing and job swaps.** An organization in Treadmill will derive great benefit—even more than when it is in Predictable Success—by using sabbaticals, job sharing, job shadowing, job swapping or any other technique that brings a fresh pair of eyes to how the organization operates.

Supreme Court Justice Louis D. Brandeis said, "Sunshine is the best disinfectant," and this statement is powerfully true for the Treadmill organization—anything that brings its increasingly stultifying systems and processes into full view and under examination is to be encouraged, and all of these practices do just that.

Coupled with the use of fixed-term postings and a new, dynamic orientation process, the use of job swaps and similar activities will ensure that employees in the Treadmill organization are deployed with fresh eyes and an inquisitive attitude. This will encourage them to challenge how systems and processes are used rather than stagnate in place, routinely going through the motions and driving the organization further toward The Big Rut.

# 3. Performance Assessment

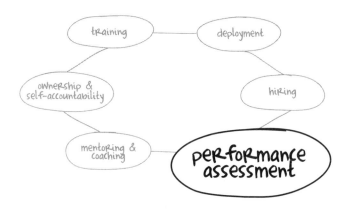

By the time the organization has reached Treadmill, there is usually one process that has come to epitomize more than any other the slavish adherence to systems and processes (in the eyes of managers and line employees alike). That process is the performance assessment, or performance review.

Burdened with page after page of metrics, dripping with impenetrable language and, above all else, attached to the reality of the employee's everyday activities by only the faintest thread of relevance, the performance assessment process of the organization in Treadmill is truly an exercise in overdependence on meretricious systems and processes. Loathed by managers for the time it takes and despised by employees for its irrelevance, it yields little of real value to management, and yet it must be performed with clockwork precision every year—quarterly for some poor souls, and in some cases, presumably in payment of heinous sins from a previous life, every month.

Okay—so maybe I've painted an extreme version of reality, but in truth, when an organization is in Treadmill, most performance assessments are tortuous and yield little in return.

It doesn't need to be that way. Undertaken correctly, there is no more motivating and useful process for an employee and manager than a truly effective performance review. But to get out of Treadmill, the entire process requires stripping down to the basics and rebuilding—otherwise it will continue to be one of the main causes of an unremitting slide toward The Big Rut.

There are three key factors in redesigning a performance assessment process to turn it from a Treadmill-enhancer to a Treadmill-killer:

**3.1 Make it success-focused.** For reasons that we don't have space to deal with here, the performance assessment process has within it an inexorable gravitational pull toward a *focus on failure*. Indeed, during Fun, a performance assessment is used only when there is a need to correct an errant employee who has in some way failed—successful employees receive little more than a slap on the back. It is from these admonitory beginnings that the use of performance assessments typically grows, and so also the tendency to focus on failure.

For the organization in Treadmill, "failure" means "failure to comply." This causes its performance assessment process to become in truth "compliance assessment": The main focus is on whether or not the employee has followed systems and processes correctly. And with that change of focus, performance assessment becomes yet another Treadmill amplification process.

To turn the performance assessment process into a tool for steering the organization back to Predictable Success, the process must first be reoriented toward success rather than failure. It should assess, for example, the use of creativity and vision rather than the failure to comply with systems and processes; it should examine and build on what was done well rather than focus on what was done poorly or was left undone.

This is not to say, of course, that the performance assessment process must be blind to failure, or that employees must be somehow sheltered from their mistakes or mollycoddled—rather that, just like a good football coach reviewing the game with his team, sharing one clip of how to make the play correctly is worth sharing ten clips of how the play was fumbled.

**3.2 Make the process a dialogue.** An organization in Treadmill can never return to Predictable Success unless and until management identifies and exploits as many opportunities as possible to engage in healthy and robust dialogue with its employees. We've already seen that the orientation process is one such opportunity, and the performance assessment process is another.

Put simply, if an employee cannot speak honestly and openly with his or her line manager about the root causes of success and failure, then no value will arise from the performance assessment process, no matter how well the paperwork is designed. Specifically for the organization in Treadmill, if managers are defensive, stoic or unengaged with their employees, and if they fail to encourage an honest and open discussion about which systems and processes contribute to the employees' success and which hinder it, then the value of the performance assessment process will be drained to the point of uselessness.

If, on the other hand, the performance assessment process is a genuine dialogue, where the employee and manager can talk openly and honestly—about not just the employee's performance, but the systems and processes he or she works with and how they can be improved—then the performance assessment process will become a major contributor to the organization's recovery.

**3.3 Make the output developmentally based.** The third change that can turn the performance assessment process into a tool for returning to Predictable Success is to make the final output from the process a personal development plan for the employee: a list of specific, actionable steps the employee can take to improve his or her performance in the period ahead, rather than just a grade or a score.

This shift of focus from the employee's degree of compliance to his or her personal development is a vital one—it sends the signal that employees will be rewarded for developing and improving over time, rather than for merely complying with systems and processes.

Turning your performance assessment process from a failure-centric, jargon-filled monologue into a success-centric dialogue focused on personal development is one of the most powerful tools in your return to Predictable Success.

# 4. Training

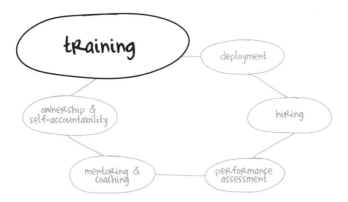

Let's recap: We're putting systems and processes together that will take the organization back to Predictable Success by helping our people manage systems and processes, rather than allowing the systems and processes to manage them.

So far we have redesigned the hiring process; learned how to effectively deploy our employees, and implemented a success-centric, personal-development focused performance assessment process. By so doing, we have ensured that we hire or promote only those employees who will contribute to a return to Predictable Success, deploy them in ways that dismantle the Treadmill "amplification effect," and focus on their personal development rather than on mere compliance with systems and processes.

The next logical step is to provide whatever training is necessary for our employees to achieve the personal development they and we are looking for. And as before, we want to do so in a way that halts the slide into Treadmill and returns us to Predictable Success, by prompting, motivating and challenging our employees to refocus on attaining *real results* rather than just compliance with systems and processes.

For an organization in Treadmill, it is not enough to simply put employees in a training room and bombard them with three-ring binders and PowerPoint presentations—in fact, doing so will almost certainly push the organization closer to The Big Rut. Just as with hiring, deployment and performance assessment, the training process needs to be re-engineered to become an effective tool in returning the organization to Predictable Success.

**4.1 Training programs need to be developmentally focused.** By the time an organization has begun the slide into Treadmill, its corporate training initiatives tend to have become sterile, rote learning exercises, where participants are expected to inhale large quantities of facts and information. The focus tends to be (as always in Treadmill) on compliance—how many sessions attended? how many topics covered?—rather than on actually attaining real results.

As we've seen many times throughout this chapter, the key to engaging employees—to recruit them in moving back to Predictable Success—is to focus on *their development*, not on simply transmitting information. If a buying officer needs to negotiate with major suppliers every year, she shouldn't attend a training program where she learns about negotiation—she should attend a program where she becomes a better negotiator. A sales rep's training program shouldn't teach him about selling—it should make him a better salesperson.

The paternalistic, monologue-based training programs that are common in Treadmill merely regurgitate the organization's approved methods and processes (thus amplifying the slide into Treadmill). Meanwhile, those focused on developing the individual independently of content constantly challenge the knowledge on which the training programs are based: Are the facts, information, systems and processes we're teaching having the required developmental effect, or not?

Answering this question honestly is a prime element of returning to Predictable Success—and doing so means moving away from appraising training programs based on one-page "happy sheets" completed by participants at the end of the training program and toward a lengthier, messier and more difficult—but infinitely more useful—appraisal based on the extent of *real change in the individual*: Did the training activity actually make the change we wanted to see, or not?

**4.2 The training must be Socratic in nature.** According to Wikipedia (at the time of writing), the Socratic method of teaching is defined thus: *A form of inquiry and debate between individuals with opposing viewpoints, based on asking and answering questions to stimulate rational thinking and to illuminate ideas.*

Contrast this with the traditional form of training in an organization in Treadmill: mostly monologues based on dry PowerPoint presentations, broken up by occasional listless "group work" that provides little real room for debate and leads participants inexorably toward a predetermined conclusion.

As we've already seen when examining orientation and performance assessment, the paternalistic monologue is death to the organization in Treadmill and will hasten its decline to The Big Rut. The training function is another area where management must replace droning subject matter experts with dynamic interaction, and dry monologues with engaging, passionate dialogue.

**4.3 The training sessions must consistently and regularly involve C-level executives.** There are two reasons why it is imperative for the C-level executives of an organization in Treadmill to participate actively and frequently in the organization's training activities:

First, no matter how intense the Socratic debate, if no one in the room has the authority and the experience to respond to the participants meaningfully, the exercise will be futile. While corporate trainers and outside experts have their place and can be useful as part of the training mix, they are no substitute for having someone in the room with the authority to actually *change* things in the organization. In fact, having a healthy debate in which changes to the organization's way of doing things are proposed *without* having someone authoritative in the room will ultimately become a frustrating and sterile exercise for the participants, who will eventually cease contributing when it becomes obvious that doing so will effect no real change.

Second, being in the bullpen with high-quality employees (now that you have changed your hiring process, you are employing only high-quality individuals, right?) is an incredibly useful source of information, feedback, ideas and energy for management—especially when the organization is in Treadmill.

Turning a tired, paternalistic, information-based training program into a developmentally focused, Socratic interchange that regularly includes C-level executives is a vitally important fourth step in returning an organization from Treadmill to Predictable Success.

# 5. Mentoring and Coaching

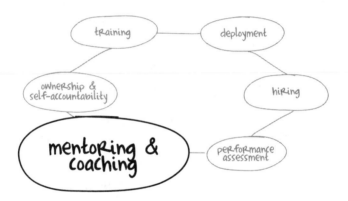

Training on its own can be a powerful tool, but its value is exponentially enhanced when it is accompanied by effective one-on-one mentoring and coaching.

Most organizations in Treadmill are large enough, and have been operating for long enough, to have mentoring and coaching programs in place. But, because the organizations are in Treadmill, usually these programs will have become robotic, formulaic—more concerned with

For the purposes of this discussion, by "coaching" we mean assisting someone with the development of functional skills, and with "mentoring" we're referring to the development of the individual as a person. Your organization may have these definitions reversed—it doesn't really matter, so long as we effectively distinguish between the two.

going through the motions than achieving lasting change for the participants.

To rejuvenate the over-managed mentoring and coaching programs in Treadmill and retool them to be effective in reversing course back to Predictable Success, three adjustments are required:

**5.1 Weed out mentors and coaches who are in it for the wrong reasons.** Overmanaged organizations in Treadmill tend to develop a subculture where brownie points are handed out to people for being seen to "do the right thing," irrespective of the individual's inner motivation. Signing up for new initiatives, heading up task forces, attending meetings—all can add to an individual's status and social currency in the Treadmill organization.

Unsurprisingly, the organization's mentoring and coaching programs aren't exempt from the impact of the brownie-point subculture, and as a result, some of the mentors and coaches will have signed up for the program more with an eye to positioning themselves within the organization, than out of a genuine desire to assist others.

While this is hardly a crime against humanity (in the Treadmill organization, signing up for something for appearances' sake is relatively normal), it is nonetheless important that management "refresh the bench" of mentors and coaches, ensuring that so far as is possible, all the mentors and coaches are genuinely engaged in the program and evince a real desire to help others. Otherwise, as we shall see in a moment, the next two steps will be very difficult to implement.

**5.2 Reduce reporting and instead encourage experimentation and exploration.** For participants, the main benefit of mentoring and coaching programs is the opportunity to "try stuff out" without fear or judgment. Whether it's being coached on how to operate a lathe or being mentored on how to be a more effective leader, the whole point of the mentoring or coaching interaction is to provide room to breathe—an environment away from the pressure of "live operations" where it's possible to try out a new skill or work on an underdeveloped attribute. In a coaching session, making a mistake on the lathe doesn't halt or slow down the production line, and in a mentoring session, a manager can experiment with different listening skills without bewildering her direct reports.

When the organization hits Treadmill, however, the pressure of compliance begins to edge out tolerance for experimentation—"trying stuff out" is the antithesis of Treadmill, which values instead the rote repetition of tried and tested routines. Mentoring and coaching sessions become monitored, metric-based and micromanaged: Is the mentee making "acceptable" progress? How many sessions did the participants have this month? How long did they meet for? What was discussed? What are the outputs from each session?

Eventually the weight of these Treadmill-typical systems and processes squeeze the lifeblood out of the mentoring and coaching sessions, and the participants—mentors and mentees, coaches and coachees alike—find themselves in an environment indistinguishable from everyday operations: no room to breathe, and limited tolerance for error or experimentation.

Even for a management team that is passionately committed to returning to Predictable Success, changing this dynamic is one of the more difficult challenges they will face. Allowing the mentoring and coaching interactions room to breathe—by reducing reporting mechanisms and instead allowing participants to experiment with their skills and explore their personal development in a risk-free and judgment-free environment—goes against the whole thrust of systems and process dependence that took the organization out of Whitewater and into Predictable Success. And yet, if the organization is to avoid declining further into the fatal grip of The Big Rut, that loosening of compliance and the reintroduction of exploration and experimentation are exactly what is required.

**5.3 Move mentoring outside the functional area and outside the line of command.** Mentoring and coaching programs work best if the participants don't have a close working relationship outside the program.

While with skills-based coaching it often isn't going to be possible to move outside the functional area to find a coach (salespeople need to coach salespeople in sales skills, lathe operators need to coach lathe operators, etc.), it should be possible to do so with mentors. In both cases, it is important to ensure that the coach or mentor is not in the coachee/mentee's upward chain of command.

This is one of the easiest ways to accelerate the shift from mentoring and coaching as a compliance-based exercise back into the realm of exploration and experiment, as it removes the performance anxiety that any coachee or mentee will naturally feel when being coached or mentored by their superior. It is very hard, if not impossible, to genuinely experiment and explore with someone you know you're going to have a performance review with at a later date.

To get from Treadmill to Predictable Success, redesign (or introduce) mentoring and coaching programs so that they involve only truly engaged mentors and coaches who have room to explore and experiment with mentees and coachees who aren't in their reporting line of command.

# 6. Ownership and Self-accountability

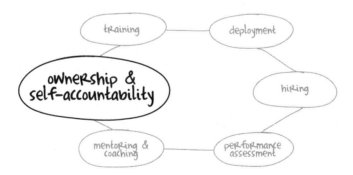

As with the transition from Whitewater to Predictable Success that we explored in the previous chapter, the shift back to Predictable Success from Treadmill is finally achieved when the cumulative changes in the other five factors (hiring, deployment, performance assessment, training, and mentoring and coaching) produce a transformation of the organization's culture of ownership and self-accountability.

You will recall that the cumulative effect of the changes made in Whitewater was to *reintroduce* a culture of ownership and self-accountability by rejuvenating the organization's mission, vision and values; realigning employees around that renewed vision; and empowering them to work cross-functionally within it.

In Treadmill the challenge is different: not to reintroduce a culture of ownership and self-accountability, but to transform an existing one. The culture of ownership and self-accountability introduced during the transition from Whitewater to Predictable Success still exists, but crucially, its focus has changed.

In Predictable Success, employees take responsibility for *outcomes*. In Treadmill, they take responsibility for *actions*. In Predictable Success, employees hold themselves accountable for *results*; in Treadmill, for *compliance*.

Thus, in Treadmill, employees take responsibility for submitting reports on time and correctly; completing checklists thoroughly and completely; and producing budgets accurately and precisely. Employees hold themselves accountable for upcoming milestones, deadlines and reporting schedules; for signing up for and attending meetings, task forces, and committees; and for consistent compliance with regulations, policies, systems and processes. So it is that in Treadmill, while the sense of ownership and self-accountability is active and flourishing (often it is an even stronger cultural imperative than when in Predictable Success), it is focused on the wrong things—on form rather than function.

Reversing the decline of Treadmill and returning to Predictable Success means, above all else, redirecting the focus of employees' ownership and self-accountability back to the attainment of real, measurable, operational results rather than the confirmation of measurable activity levels. And, as with the rejuvenation of ownership and self-accountability in Whitewater, this cannot be mandated—the nature of ownership and self-accountability is that it comes from within.

Instead, when an organization makes effective changes in the five preceding areas, the cumulative result will be a shift in each individual's focus of ownership and self-accountability back to achieving real, measurable outputs, not just complying with systems and processes:

1. **Hiring:** We've redesigned the hiring process so we are hiring and promoting only those who focus on results, not just activity levels.

2. **Deployment:** Beginning with orientation and continuing with fixed-term positions, job swapping and similar programs, we have encouraged employees to focus on real results and to look to their own development—not the maintenance of a specific position in the organization—as their key goal.

3. **Performance assessment:** We have consistently and regularly provided employees with a success-centric, development-focused dialogue about how they are performing, and we have clearly identified the improvements they can make in their own performance.

4. **Training:** Once those developmental opportunities have been identified, we have provided appropriate training in the form of a developmentally focused, Socratic interchange that regularly includes C-level executives and that challenges employees to effect real change in their individual performance, not just the accumulation of information.

5. **Mentoring and coaching:** Corporate training has been augmented with mentoring and coaching programs that provide access to truly engaged mentors and coaches who have room to explore and experiment with the mentees and coachees.

The individual effect of these five major changes is to cleanse the organization of "dead zones"—those areas where mere compliance is an acceptable performance standard—replacing them instead with a focus on individual personal development.

The *cumulative* effect is to transform the organization's culture of ownership and self-accountability, away from a focus on compliance and activity levels, and back where it belongs: focusing on outcomes and results.

When this happens—and not before—the organization will have not only halted the slide from Treadmill to The Big Rut, but successfully returned to Predictable Success.

## SUMMARY

- To move from Treadmill back into Predictable Success, management needs to make six specific changes to the way in which it manages the people in the organization.

- First, it must redesign its hiring process to ensure that it is hiring only those who will contribute to a return to Predictable Success, not those who will keep the organization in Treadmill.

- Second, the way in which employees are deployed must be changed to shake the organization out of its overdependence on systems and processes.

- Third, the performance assessment process must be revamped to focus on development and success, rather than on failure and compliance.

- Fourth, the corporate training function must be turned from an information delivery vehicle into a dynamic dialogue of exploration into how and why to do things better.

- Fifth, mentoring and coaching programs must be relieved of overmanagement and freed to allow experimentation and exploration of skills and attributes.

- Sixth, as a result of the first five steps, ownership and self-accountability will be redirected away from a focus on compliance and activity levels and toward outputs and real results, providing the final push back to Predictable Success.

# [ CHAPTER ELEVEN ]

## STAYING AT THE PEAK: MAINTAINING PREDICTABLE SUCCESS ONCE YOU GET THERE

"Together we're unlimited. Together we'll be the greatest team."
—Stephen Schwartz, "Defying Gravity," from the musical *Wicked*

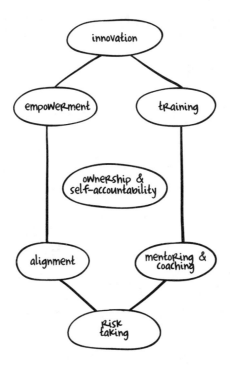

AS WILL BE OBVIOUS BY NOW, GETTING TO (AND MORE PARTICU-larly, remaining in) Predictable Success is not a one-off event. The bal-ance—between, on the one hand, maintaining the systems and processes needed to keep the organization from slipping back into Whitewater, and on the other, avoiding pushing the organization into Treadmill by over-cooking those systems and processes—is a delicate one, and one that, given the nature of business, shifts daily. A management team that is complacent about its Predictable Success status will soon find it slipping away.

In theory, however, there is no reason why an organization should not remain in Predictable Success forever, or—more likely—for a very long time (changes in external factors such as technology, legislation and the environment will catch up with most organizations at some point). So long as management is flexible and alert to the ever-changing shifts in emphasis needed to keep the balance between systems and processes on the one hand, and vision, entrepreneurial zeal and risk taking on the other, the organization can—and will—remain in Predictable Success indefinitely. Doing so involves two steps.

# Step One: Installing and Maintaining Two Balancing Systems

Keeping the organization in Pre-dictable Success involves first installing, then actively maintain-ing the systems and processes out-lined in the previous two chapters.

Obviously, both sets of sys-tems and processes are necessary—the more mechanical systems and processes outlined in Chapter 9, which build the machine for deci-sion making that takes the organi-zation out of Whitewater, and the rather more dynamic, people-oriented

> Because staying in Predictable Suc-cess involves installing and main-taining the systems and processes needed to get out of Treadmill, very few organizations achieve lasting Predictable Success on their first "visit"—most need to spend time in Treadmill in order to see the need for (and implement) the second, "people" set of systems and processes.

systems and processes of Chapter 10, which prevent the organization are overdoing it and sliding into Treadmill.

The two sets of systems and processes are complementary, together creating a constructive tension in the way the organization works—adhering to systems, but also encouraging individual initiative and focusing on results, not just activity levels. Taken together, they result in a strong, vibrant culture of results-focused ownership and self-accountability throughout the organization, which is the lynchpin of Predictable Success.

Figure 11.1: Ownership and Self-accountability—the Lynchpin to Achieving Systems Balance in Predictable Success

# Step Two: Institutionalizing Innovation and Risk Taking

For the organization to maintain its position in Predictable Success over the long-term, one more thing needs to be accomplished: The organization must develop its own innate ability to innovate and take risks—those entrepreneurial attributes that until now it has depended upon the founder/owners or individual members of senior management to deliver.

The reason this is important is that unless and until innovation and risk taking are part of the warp and woof of the organization—part of how it thinks and acts on a daily basis—it will be vulnerable to the loss of its entrepreneurial, visionary zeal at any time, should the key individual(s) who embody those attributes choose to leave.

Now of course, the reality is that an "organization" cannot develop innate skills on its own—the organization is an inanimate object. What we're really talking about is driving the ability to innovate and take appropriate risk down into the organization—through its people. In other words, rather than viewing innovation and risk taking as some form of magic spell exercised by only the chosen few, management instead turns the ability to innovate and take appropriate risk into skills practiced by the workforce as a whole.

This can be a difficult challenge for management, for two reasons. The first reason is that sometimes, particularly if the founder/owners are still around, being the possessor of an entrepreneurial "magic spell" is a key part of management's identity, and one that they can be loath to share. When this is the case, there may be little that can be done, and the organization will experience Predictable Success only for so long as the founder/owners remain actively engaged in the business. Sadly, this often happens to family companies, with the first generation handing over to the second (or third), only to find that the magic spell wasn't transferred in the family DNA.

The second reason that institutionalizing innovation and risk taking can be difficult for management is fear: fear that the employees will use such powerful tools unwisely, taking risks and/or innovating in ways that will harm the company rather than benefit it.

This fear is understandable and not unwarranted—however, the systems and processes put in place by Step One above provide the answer. By linking both innovation and risk taking to our existing systems and processes in the right way, we can harness their enormous potential throughout the organization, without betting the farm.

## 1. RISK TAKING.

Let's look at risk taking first, as management typically has more fear of its misuse than that of innovation.

Management's fear of "institutionalizing" risk taking is understandable and simple: Getting it wrong can threaten the organization's very existence. We don't have to look very far back in corporate history to see examples of sometimes massive companies that were completely (or almost completely) extinguished because of undue risk taking by employees. In the aftermath of Bear Sterns and Lehman Brothers, who wouldn't think twice about delegating the authority to take substantive risks beyond the senior management team?

And yet, as we've seen, to build an organization that will remain in Predictable Success, it needs to be done.

As pointed out above, the answer lies in managing the risk taking process by linking it to the other systems and processes we already have in place. Specifically, this means corralling and regulating risk taking activities, so that they operate only in those areas and in a manner that we know will benefit the organization (by making it more entrepreneurial and flexible) without damaging it (by exposing it to undue, unwise or unnecessary risk).

Specifically, we manage risk taking by linking it directly to alignment, and to mentoring and coaching:

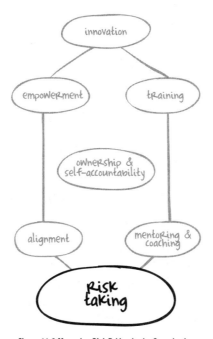

Figure 11.2 Managing Risk Taking in the Organization

By doing this, we ensure two things: First, by constraining risk taking so that it can take place only in alignment with the organization's mission, vision and values, we set clear boundaries. No wild bets on products, services or activities that aren't part of our core business; no engaging in any activities antithetical to our core values; no going "off the reservation"; and no acting as a loose cannon or maverick.

Second, by insisting that risk taking is always and only exercised within the constraints of a transparent and open mentoring and/or coaching relationship, we ensure that there is always supportive oversight for the risk taking activity from a more experienced mentor or coach, and that no employee can expose the organization to risk on his or her own say-so.

## 2. INNOVATION.

Let's turn now to innovation—an integral element in institutionalizing entrepreneurial zeal and vision throughout the organization.

Here, management is typically concerned less with the possibility of "betting the farm" and risking the organization's existence than it is with simply wasting time, energy, money and resources by allowing employees to chase inappropriate, impracticable or simply harebrained ideas.

Again, management's fears are reasonable and not unwarranted. And again, the answer lies in managing the innovation process by linking it to the systems and processes we already have in place—that is, corralling and regulating the innovation process so that it operates only within those areas and in a manner that we know will benefit the organization without consuming untoward resources.

In this case, we manage innovation by linking it directly to both empowerment and training (see Figure 11.3).

By doing this we again achieve two things: First, by linking innovation directly to only those areas in which the individual(s) have been explicitly empowered to act (either individually within their functional area or as part of a cross-functional team), we ensure that innovation is being applied only to genuine challenges faced by the organization—not harebrained or inappropriate projects.

Second, by providing all employees with access to high-quality, developmental training on how to innovate effectively, we reduce the potential for redundancy and inefficiency in the innovation process.

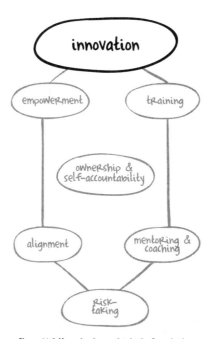

Figure 11.3 Managing Innovation in the Organization

## 3. THE SAFETY NET OF THE WHOLE FRAMEWORK.

Although we achieve primary control over innovation and risk taking by linking them to specific elements in the existing systems and processes as detailed above, they are also positively impacted by other elements of the Predictable Success framework. Our restructured hiring process, for example, will bring in people who are proven innovators and risk takers, and the performance management process will identify and root out inappropriate activities in either area. Cross-functional teams provide boundaries and oversight for risk taking that complement the mentoring and coaching process, and the fixed terms of our deployment process nourishes innovation by ensuring that fresh eyes are applied to every aspect of the organization's activities on a regular basis.

# The lynchpin of Predictable Success: Ownership and Self-accountability

So now we have completed the three phases necessary to build an organization that gets to—and stays in—Predictable Success:

*First*, installing the decision-making systems and processes necessary to move the organization out of Whitewater and into Predictable Success;

*Second*, installing the "people" systems and processes needed to bring the organization back out of Treadmill and once more into Predictable Success; and

*Third*, institutionalizing innovation and risk taking throughout the organization.

The final result looks like this:

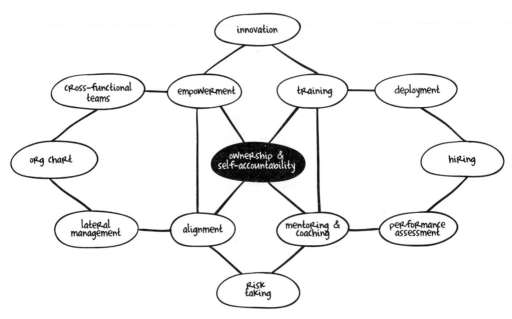

Figure 11.4 The Complete Predictable Success Framework

As we've seen so often previously, the lynchpin of the entire framework comes down to personal ownership and self-accountability throughout the organization: engaged, empowered individuals and teams who hold themselves accountable for delivering real results, and who exercise structured creativity, innovation and risk taking to achieve *their* goals, which are also *your* goals.

## SUMMARY

- An organization may move in and out of Predictable Success (to Whitewater or Treadmill) many times, but it can "lock in" Predictable Success and stay there for a prolonged period.

- To do so, it must first implement, then maintain the decision-making systems and processes needed to get from Whitewater to Predictable Success and the people-related systems and processes needed to move back into Predictable Success from Treadmill.

- This means that an organization is more likely to remain in Predictable Success if it has experienced a time in Treadmill.

- Additionally, the organization must institutionalize innovation and risk taking, pushing it down throughout the organization.

- Management can mitigate the risks involved in doing so by linking innovation and risk taking to specific elements of the Predictable Success framework.

- The lynchpin of Predictable Success is the existence of a healthy culture of ownership and self-accountability, with employees focused on delivering real results and exercising structured creativity, innovation and risk taking to achieve their goals, which are also your goals.

# INDEX

# ACKNOWLEDGMENTS

This book exists primarily because of the patience of executives in hundreds of companies who have allowed me to work with them over the last thirty years. To all of you, my deepest thanks. It amazes me that you pay me to learn, and I appreciate the privilege.

Apart from my clients, four men (yes, all men—I wish it were otherwise, but it isn't) have at one time or another profoundly impacted how I think about life in general and business in particular: Jim, William, Ronnie, and Will. Thank you.

There is already a profound if limited body of work on the life cycles of organizations, and informed readers will appreciate that Part 1 of this book stands on the shoulders of the thinking and writing of many others, not least Ichak Adizes, Daniel S. Rippy, Richard Foster, Michael Gerber, and Lawrence M. Miller.

Christopher Alexander's extraordinary book *A Pattern Language: Towns, Buildings, Construction* fueled my desire to write a book that explains how business works as eloquently and as simply as his explains everything else.

Julie Wilson, my terrifyingly brilliant wife, made me do it.

# ABOUT THE AUTHOR

Les McKeown is the president & CEO of Predictable Success.

With over twenty-five years of global business experience, including starting forty-two companies in his own right, and as the founding partner of an incubation consulting company that launched hundreds of businesses worldwide, Les has an intuitive understanding of why businesses grow and succeed.

Les's clients have included Harvard University, the US Army, Pella Corporation, Chiron Corporation, Microsoft, United Technologies Corporation, the Canadian Defence Department, MI-SWACO, St. Vincent Health, VeriSign, and many others.

Les has appeared on CNN, ABC and the BBC, and in *USA Today* and the *New York Times*. He lives in Marblehead, Massachusetts, with his wife and two dogs, and receives occasional care packages from his three children.

# LET'S GO! FIVE RESOURCES TO HELP YOU GET STARTED WITH PREDICTABLE SUCCESS

Are you ready to take your journey to Predictable Success? If so, here are the essential resources you need to get started:

**1. Access the Book-Owners-Only Resources.**
Additional resources just for you:
http://PredictableSuccess.com/book/resources

**2. Read the Predictable Success Blog.**
Get free tools, tips and techniques to accelerate and deepen your Predictable Success, right at your desktop:
http://PredictableSuccess.com/blog/

**3. Join the Predictable Success Community.**
Join the Predictable Success online community and connect with us using your favorite social media network:
Twitter: http://PredictableSuccess.com/Twitter
Facebook: http://PredictableSuccess.com/Facebook
LinkedIn: http://PredictableSuccess.com/LinkedIn
YouTube: http://PredictableSuccess.com/YouTube

**4. Take the Predictable Success Quiz.**
Want to know what stage in the journey to Predictable Success your organization, group or team is at? Take the free Predictable Success Quiz at: http://PredictableSuccess.com/Quiz

**5. Accelerate into Predictable Success.**

The Predictable Success Workshop is by far the easiest—and fastest—way to accelerate your path to Predictable Success. Spend two days with Les McKeown and take away a detailed, immediately implement-able Predictable Success action plan—entirely customized to your organization's (or your division's, department's, group's or team's) specific situation.

Les will personally guide you, together with an elite group* of other executives exactly like you, through the Predictable Success process, enabling you to:

- Pinpoint exactly where you are on the Predictable Success life cycle.

- Identify precisely what the barriers are for your organization in getting to Predictable Success.

- Construct a detailed, highly effective action plan listing the precise steps you need to take to get to Predictable Success.

- Agree on an accountability process that powerfully increases the implementation of your Predictable Success "back at the ranch."

See complete details of the Predictable Success Workshop and sign up here: http://PredictableSuccess.com/workshop.

---

* To ensure that Les can provide detailed, personal coaching, the Predictable Success Workshop is restricted to just twenty participants from noncompeting organizations.